Also by Dr. Cheri L. Florance:

* *BE ME: Brain Engineering Of My Emotions*, in press, Brain Science Publishing, 2009

* *AMP Up With The Animals: AMPlify Attention-Memory-Processing*, Brain Science Publishing, 2009

* *The Maverick Mind,* Penguin Books, 2004

* *A Boy Beyond Reach,* Simon & Schuster, 2004

* *Stutter-Free Speech*, Charles E. Merrill Publishing, 1980

Autism: A New Hope

Unlocking The Mysteries
Of The Maverick Mind

How one parent and her son surmounted the odds and turned an "unteachable" child into a reachable student and family member, and beyond—and what other parents can do when faced with a similar situation.

by

Cheri L. Florance, Ph.D.

With excerpts from *Cheri Florance, Ph.D.,*
The Brain Storms of A Brain Scientist Ahead Of Her Time

by Joseph L. Tatner

Published by Brain Science Publishing
160 Riverside Boulevard, New York, NY 10069.
Email address: braindr@cheriflorance.com

Authors: Cheri L. Florance, Ph.D., with excepts from
Cheri Florance, Ph.D., The Brain Storms of A Brain Scientist Ahead Of Her Time
by Joseph L. Tatner

Art & Design: Missy Rinaldi
Editor: Margaret Daisley

Printed in 2009

ISBN: 978-0-578-03346-4

I would like to dedicate this book to my three wonderful children—*Vanessa*, now a Manhattan Attorney, who, always the manager, was engaged in the strategic planning for discovering new hope for autism from the young age of 3, helping me implement her brother's very innovative and creative program; *William*, a chemical engineer, who travels the world to trouble shoot and solve process engineering problems for big business, was analyzing the process engineering of the human brain when he was in pre-school, helping me with Head Start children; and *Whitney,* who walked the walk through the journey of Maverick and who also uses his highly visual brain as a chemical engineer, brilliant at solving physics and high-level big-picture cognitive problems, just like Dr. Albert Einstein.

I would also like to acknowledge writer and author Joseph Tatner, who was able to research and organize a great amount of material, expanding on my original concept to present an informative, positive message of hope.

.

 # A special thanks to:

Joseph L. Tatner is a professional writer and researcher with a B.A. in Communications, an M.A. in Political Science, and a teaching credential from the State of California. He takes a personal interest in Dr. Florance's research and its message of hope to all parents with children facing the challenges of autism.

Missy Rinaldi is trained in both fine art and digital/graphic arts, and truly loves creating design, but says she works just as much at being a mom to two fabulous, active kids. Ms. Rinaldi recently moved to Virginia, after living in Southern California for 21 years, to be near parents and open a restaurant—which has given her interior sense of design a flex. Three years later, Sirena Cucina Italiana is a fabulous success, thanks to her wonderful husband and a fabulous clientele. She invites you to stop by when you're in Norfolk.

Margaret Daisley has been an editor in New York City since 1996, focusing on non-fiction books, articles and research reports. She has an M.A. in English from the University of Massachusetts, Amherst and a B.A. in American Studies from Queens College, City University of New York. Nothing pleases her more than helping to nurture a project from inception to publication, especially one as worthwhile as this book.

Table of Contents

Table of Contents

 # Forward

When Dr. Florance originally contacted me, it was to combine a series of articles into a book that would accompany her video. However, it quickly developed into something much more. We had similar backgrounds in theatre and although I had nowhere near the medical or psychological training she had, I had enough understanding of psychology and the scientific method to understand her work. Moreover, my heart went out to her and all those who bravely faced the unknown to fight for their children. I felt for her son and all outside the mainstream who are labeled as "defective" in some way by those who fail to understand.

My own personal history included being labeled a social misfit, and I was tested in grammar school to find out what was "wrong" with me that caused other kids to pick on me. The obvious fact that I was the smallest kid in the class with big nerd glasses that made my ears stick out never seemed to offer a clue to my teachers as to why bigger kids might beat me up. It turned out that in 5th grade, my IQ was that of a sophomore in high school and there was no way the kids in my class and I could relate to each other. I was your quintessential geek, building science models like *The Visible Man* instead of model hot rods at home, so my peers and I were on completely different levels with no common ground for communication or understanding.

As a single father raising a beautiful little girl, I have devoured a vast amount of material on fatherhood, parenting and childhood development. My heart was touched by the stories of parents bravely facing incredible challenges. My child has thankfully been spared such challenges, but I have interacted with mentally disabled children and my father used to teach music to the blind. My cousin was born with Down's syndrome and his family took care of him in their own home, despite the difficulties involved. I understand the gut-wrenching emotions that come into play when your child is suffering and you feel powerless to help. As I learned more about Dr. Florance, her patients and her work, I became determined to make this book more than just a compilation of scientific facts gathered over the years to augment other information. I knew this book had to scream out to struggling parents, "Yes, there is hope!" I am grateful to Dr. Florance for allowing me the opportunity to be a part of this endeavor.

Regarding the visual brain, I remember one incident at a shopping mall. Out of nowhere, at age 2, my daughter started shouting, "Memo! Memo!" This was her word for "Nemo," the little fish in the Disney movie. I looked all over and it took a minute for me to figure out what she was talking about. About 50 yards away was a large balloon display, the kind with small Mylar balloons stuck on a stick. Over a hundred balloons were sticking out of the central "tree" on display and there was *one* little Nemo balloon somewhere in the middle. Sure enough, that's what she had spotted.

 *Forward*

This was similar to other instances where my daughter would call out, "Mickey!" or some other cartoon character. If I didn't see it at first, I knew that if I looked around long enough, I'd find what she was looking at, or I'd turn her loose from her stroller and she'd go straight to whatever it was that had stuck out clearly to her, but which I had completely missed. Reading Dr. Florance's research and personal story on "Opticoders," I understood what would happen if this ability was amplified to a super-human ability to the detriment of verbal ability. I also understood what could happen if my little girl wanted to get closer to the Nemo balloon, but had no language skills to tell me so. She could have had a fit or started crying from frustration and I would have had no idea why.

While no one can guarantee that any particular child will be helped, since each child has his or her own unique abilities and challenges, Dr. Florance has helped thousands of children and adults over the last 40 years to prove that many who were thought "unteachable" were able to break through their individual challenges to lead symptom-free lives. This book explains why Dr. Florance is not selling snake oil or offering false hope. The old maxim, "If it sounds too good to be true, it probably is" really doesn't apply, because there are clear examples of Dr. Florance's success. The critic might argue, "Well, those kids weren't really autistic anyway, or they never would have been able to improve." Even if we assume that is true, those children were still *diagnosed* with autism and their parents were still in despair. Others might say I am not a full-time scientist so I am not equipped to evaluate the data. Fair enough, but the finest professionals in the field who *are* qualified have evaluated and endorsed her work, giving her great praise from all over the world.

In summary, this book was not written as an academic work for publication in a medical journal. The science and theory is included, but it is written as much for the heart as for the brain. The target audience is the individual parent and family member, not the medical expert. Dr. Florance has numerous publications in medical journals for those who want more detailed scientific information on her studies.

This book is about a woman who would not let her son be labeled a permanent failure, and about the hope she offers to other parents in similar situations.

—*Joseph L. Tatner*

A Mother's Journey of Irony and Fate

Dr. Cheri L. Florance is an internationally recognized brain scientist, professor, clinical researcher and author who has a long track record of helping a wide variety of people with communication disorders, behavioral problems and autism. Her story is filled with irony and "coincidences" that seemed to predestine her to be the mother of a little boy who would be diagnosed with such maladies as autism and severe mental retardation. That little boy, named Whitney, recently graduated from college with a degree in chemical engineering and is completely symptom free, thanks to the mother who refused to give up. She found the key to unlock his mind to the rest of the world – a key which everyone else had missed.

Dr. Florance's multi-disciplinary training and unique experiences enabled her to pick up on clues from her own child that lab research alone could never have discovered. She had to find a way to reach her son. Failure was not an option.

Specializing in treatment of the neurological aspects of communication, Dr. Florance has pioneered innovative treatment methods since 1969 to improve attention, listening, speaking, reading, writing and memory skills. Dr. Florance began her private practice in 1975. Since then, she has helped literally thousands of people around the world and is an internationally recognized expert who offers parents real hope for their children.

Dr. Florance has earned numerous honors for her work over the years. She was one of the youngest people ever to be named a Fellow by The American Speech-Language-Hearing Association (ASHA), an award given to less than 1% of its members. She received the Distinguished Service to Mankind Award from Muskingum College. She has been invited to present more than 200 workshops at hospitals, universities, and national meetings, and has set up programs in school districts throughout the United States. She has served on national panels and committees and was an editor of *The Journal of Speech, Language, and Hearing Research*.

Her office has been selected many times by test developers and corporations as a field site for new tests and equipment. CBS News, *Oprah*, *The Today Show*, *Hour Magazine*, *P.M. Magazine*, *USA Today*, and numerous other newspapers, magazines, and news programs have interviewed Dr. Florance. The Mayor of Columbus, the Governor of Ohio and the White House have all honored her.

Dr. Florance receives the prestigious
Distinguished Service Award from
Muskingum College Alumni Association

Dr. Florance was born in 1948. She grew up in a family of professional musicians and began performing herself at the tender age of 3. Little Cheri's Mom was an accomplished symphony musician, so the child grew up surrounded and influenced by music. Her mom's best friend owned a dance studio and began teaching Cheri ballet at age 3.

By the time she was in the 7th grade, the owner/teacher asked Cheri to help teach dance classes after school. The teacher had her few favorites in the class and preferred to focus her attention on the children that seemed naturally gifted. She was frustrated by the kids who didn't quite "get it" and asked Cheri to teach them. Even at age 12, Cheri found it ironic that she, the young 7th grader, was asked to teach the students with difficulties while the "professional" only taught the easy students.

Cheri took the slow learners down to the basement. She noticed that some children had difficulty following directions, sequencing steps, processing information and staying on task. Instinctively, she figured out that she needed to break each step down into parts. She watched the students, taught them slowly, and then practiced with them until they were up to speed. When everyone knew the routine, she would bring them back to the studio to rejoin the other students. She felt great compassion for these students and worked hard to make sure they loved to dance as much as she did.

Young Cheri saw firsthand how children who didn't process information at the same speed as the rest of a group felt isolated and sad. Frustration often led to crying and temper tantrums. Even at that young age, Cheri saw firsthand how separating kids only made them feel they were in "the stupid class," and something about that was just wrong. Inspired by her grandfather's experience as a musician, writer, researcher, inventor, and educator, Cheri began studying how children decode information to self-instruct a motor response. Before long, she was putting that research into practice facing a new challenge.

An 8-year-old boy came into the dance studio who wanted to learn to tap dance. Ordinarily, the teacher would have been happy to teach him herself, but this little boy was different. This little boy was blind.

The teacher gave the boy to Cheri for private lessons in the studio. This was quite a step up from the basement, and they worked together when other classes were not going on. Cheri's patience and persistence in teaching the other kids paid off and she was able to break down the steps slowly, moving his feet with her hands so he could hear the sounds he was making, match the sounds that she was making, and build muscle memory. She taught him for four years until she finished high school.

Dr. Florance's father studied aeronautical engineering, served as a Navy fighter pilot and became a commercial pilot. She helped him work on airplanes and he taught her to fly. This experience taught her to think in mechanical terms with logic and precision. Unlike the art form of dance, however, learning to fly was counter-intuitive for Cheri. The visual-mechanical thinking of her father was very different from her way of thinking in words and paragraphs.

Her dad seemed perplexed by how hard it was for her to learn to fly. He wondered why an honor student who learned so easily in school would have such a hard time absorbing what seemed so natural to him. "I have taught thousands of Navy pilots," he thought. "Why can't she learn this?" Now the tables were turned, and it was Cheri who needed someone to help her with a difficult brain task she didn't quite understand. He did help her—as she had helped the dance students—with a lot of patience. She completed her first solo flight on her 16th birthday.

When she went on to college, Cheri continued to get good grades and majored in French and Communication. She lived in Paris in the French Honors House where no English was spoken. Learning a foreign language helped her understand even more deeply about the intricacies of language and communication.

As a Liberal Arts major, she was a soloist in the choir, a choreographer, an athlete on her school's competitive synchronized swim team, and an actress. She wanted to pursue an acting career but in a truly unbelievable twist of fate, Cheri was frustrated when she wanted to take an advanced acting class. The school required that students complete a class in speech and hearing disorders. Unable to see how that had anything to do with acting, she went to the Dean to ask for a waiver so she wouldn't have to take the class, saying, "I have no use for this class! I don't want to be a speech disorder therapist, I want to *act*!" The Dean agreed she made a very good argument, but told her she had to take the class anyway.

Cheri Florance,
as a college student.

Despite her initial reluctance, the class was taught by one of the acting class teachers and he made it so enjoyable, she asked to do an independent study afterward. Fate played yet another bizarre trick on Cheri when she was told to research "childhood aphasia." Cheri went to the library but forgot the word she was told. She knew it was something that started with an "A," so she began reading on "autism." Cheri was intrigued by the stories of children who seemed locked away in their own little world, unable to communicate or to be reached.

Armed with a pile of books after hours of reading, she returned to her teacher with the news that she had gathered the material for her research on autism. The teacher informed her of the mistake and noted the "fact" that autism was *not* a speech or hearing disorder. It was a mental illness, thought at that time to be a special form of schizophrenia. Sure enough, the books all belonged to the mental health section of the library. The young college student (not having the formal training to know any better) couldn't understand how autism could be classified as a mental health disorder when the problem was obviously one of communication: the children did not speak and did not seem to be able to hear. Since she had done so much research already, Cheri was allowed to write her independent study on autism despite this obvious "error" on her part.

The 20-year-old college student learned about her "error" in the first article she read: the 1965 *Life Magazine* article, "Screams, Slaps and Love," which outlined the predominant treatment at the time for autism. The article explained the need to slap autistic kids to get them to talk. If slapping and screaming at the child didn't work, the electric shock room was always available. This Applied Behavioral Analysis method was started in UCLA, developed by Dr. Ivar Lovaas, and (in a revised format) is still one of the primary methods used even today. The treatment typically can cost up to $100,000 per child.

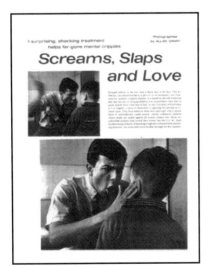

"Screams, Slaps and Love,"
Life Magazine, May 7, 1965.

Cheri became fascinated by the topic of autism. She applied to the Speech and Hearing science program at Ohio State University and was offered a scholarship for the graduate school. The only problem was that she was still only a Junior at Muskingum College. OSU didn't mind, so she actually completed an accelerated curriculum to earn both her bachelor's and master's degrees at the age of 21.

Cheri was awarded a U.S. Rehabilitation Services Commission Scholarship. Accepting this grant required her to spend 20 hours per week working with adults who had serious communication problems such as laryngectomy, stuttering, foreign accent intelligibility problems, and auditory processing and language disorders.

While in graduate school, she thought, "What if I wrote music and designed plays for kids who don't talk, using improvisation and creative dramatics and singing songs?" She wrote her Master's thesis on "Creative Dramatics and Creative Music to Help Children with Language," and created a study that included students at two kindergartens. At one school she taught songs, played guitar and involved the kids in plays and improvisation. The other school was the control group so she did not use such methods. When she compared the results, she found that music and drama helped the children talk in longer sentences, articulate more clearly and listen with better accuracy.

After receiving her Master's Degree, Cheri Florance was awarded a special job in Memphis, Tennessee working for the U.S. Dept of Education. She was in for quite a culture shock. The hospitality and beauty of the South impressed her, but she had to get used to the many cultural differences, including being branded "the Yankee." This experience helped her later understand what it must be like for someone to be a "stranger in a strange land" where they don't quite fit in, and how difficult it could be to speak the same language yet not be able to communicate effectively. George Bernard Shaw once wrote, "England and America are two countries separated by a common language." Cheri felt the same way in Memphis.

In 1970, Cheri received a pre-doctoral research fellowship from the U.S. Department of Education. As a research assistant to Dr. John V. Irwin, an expert in experimental psychology, she implemented his protocols in school districts located in Mississippi, Tennessee and Arkansas. Cheri was responsible for supervising 10 graduate student trainees as they used new teaching machines and video training to correct communication disorders. She also learned the use of psycholinguistic tests to evaluate auditory and visual processing skills under the supervision of Dr. Donald Ramp, Ph.D., and how to use the Myers-Briggs and Rogerian counseling methods under Ms. Louise Ward.

Cheri was hired to identify high-risk students so they could be directed into special programs. Many grad students had come back from the Vietnam War so they were much older than Cheri, who was now their boss. Cheri and her team were assigned to set up programs in the Mississippi Delta where children haphazardly attended school due to an absence of mandatory education laws. She learned the hard way how to set up programs and perform research in very unusual environments.

At this point, Cheri realized she had a lot more to learn and decided to pursue a double doctorate, one in Speech and Hearing and the other in Psychology. Despite the prevailing literature, she instinctively knew there was a crossover between communication disabilities and behavioral problems that manifested themselves in autism. She clearly saw a relation that no one else did. She had to prove it. She had no way of knowing that she would have an autistic child of her own one day.

While working on her doctorate, she also started to publish articles on the research projects she created. Using patients from Riverside and University Hospitals, Cheri learned the Mayo Clinic procedures for measuring attention, memory and processing under the supervision of Jon L. Deal, Ph.D. In 1972, at the age of 24, Cheri Florance was awarded a doctoral scholarship to serve as Director of the Ohio State University Speech and Hearing Clinic. She was responsible for all faculty or student service delivery for the next three years. She developed and supervised student training programs throughout the city and the Central Ohio area for all Master and Doctoral level students.

From 1972 to 1975, she created research projects that became her doctoral dissertation in Psycholinguistics (how children learn language). This was partially supported by a research grant awarded by The Ohio Department of Maternal and Child Health. Because she was enrolled in a dual degree program, professors from both the Departments of Psychology and Speech Pathology supervised her doctoral degree. She completed academic requirements for licensure in both areas, but she chose to limit her practice to the treatment of communication disorders.

Analyzing the verbal behaviors of preschool children in response to teacher instructions, Cheri received a three-year clinical mentoring grant to supervise five graduate students in rural Ohio, providing speech and language rehabilitation to underprivileged elementary school children. She used her work with normally developing preschoolers to help her design programs for the delayed patients. Later, she replicated her studies with older children and college students. Decoding language in the classroom turned out to be the key to academic success.

From 1975 to 1978, working for the U.S. Rehabilitation Services Commission, Dr. Florance pioneered "The Florance Therapy Paradigm." The phases in the therapy combined learning theory with client-centered counseling. The merging of these two divergent strategies led to improved therapies for articulation, attention, memory, language, stuttering, dyslexia and aphasia. She was assigned 12 graduate trainees as part of this project. Much of the patient care funding was from federal and state Bureaus of Vocational Rehabilitation.

Dr. Florance established the Communication Disorders Institute [CDI] at St. Anthony Medical Center (SAMC) as a private practice in 1975. Over the next 12 years, the practice increased to a staff of 25, including occupational, physical, speech and creative arts therapists, as well as social workers, psychologists and audiologists. Housed in a renovated parochial school on the SAMC campus, CDI offered both inpatient and outpatient care. Programs were provided to Head Start, Catholic schools, The Head Start program included 600 children per year. The biggest problem, however, was that many of the kids didn't show up. This impressed upon Dr. Florance the genuine need for consistency with any of the treatment options. Children who consistently attended improved, while those who did not showed less — if any — real improvement. In fact, the schedule turned out to be one of the most critical predictors of a successful outcome.

In the late 70's, Dr. Florance helped design computer systems that could speak and biofeedback devices to boost auditory processing for corporations in the Silicon Valley. These corporations hired her to create multimedia presentations and keynote addresses in the high tech corporate world.

Dr. Florance sets up her "teletrainer" equipment in 1976

She was working on yet another research project when her boss (a Palestinian Arab) asked if she would like to go to Pakistan on a goodwill mission. It was to be sort of a foreign exchange program for American and Pakistani doctors. Encountering Mississippi after a lifetime in Ohio turned out to be more of a cultural change than traveling to Pakistan. As an Ambassador for the United States, Dr. Florance was to learn about the other country and share intellectual ideas with all the heads of state. Unfortunately, the Pakistani government was overthrown just before she and her party arrived. Pakistan was now a military state. She was treated very hospitably and was able to meet with the former President (who was in jail) and the new leaders.

Exposed to yet another completely new culture and new ways of thinking, new ways to communicate, and different educational systems, this experience added to her global insight that has proved invaluable, considering she now works with clients in Greece, Moscow, Poland, South Africa, United Kingdom — literally all over the world. These experiences also later allowed her to better understand her own son who would seem like he was "from another planet."

In 1978, Dr. Florance earned a five-year Teacher Investigator Award from the National Institutes of Health (NIH). Supervised by the internationally recognized clinical psychologist, Dr. George H. Shames, Dr. Florance was rigorously trained in the methods of psychotherapy and psychometric intelligence testing. This five-year training program offered her a unique and exciting educational experience. Dr. Shames and Dr. Florance published many articles, book chapters and teaching materials together. Their book, *Stutter Free Speech*, is considered a classic work on the therapeutic relationship and operant conditioning.

In her NIH work, Dr. Florance evaluated psychometric and observational test protocols. She studied the role of brain science in communication, intelligence and personality, as well as copying and defense mechanicals. Working with Dr. Shames, she developed the Coping and Compliance Assessment (CCA) for predicting prognosis. She gave the CCA to hundreds of stutterers and surgical patients in order to plan their treatment.

Dr. Florance works to alleviate stuttering using delayed auditory feedback equipment.

Dr. Florance was then asked to design research with vascular surgeon William Evans to investigate the effects of altered carotid and cerebral blood flow on cognition, attention, processing and memory. Endarterectomy patients were measured with I.Q., voice and language tests. Questionnaires were given to patients and families to determine changes in thinking or communicating after blood flow to the brain was altered or increased.

In 1983, Dr. Florance created the Center for Independent Living (CIL), the geriatric rehabilitation unit at SAMC. The patients were tested in simulated living labs built right inside the hospital, including a Huntington Bank, Big Bear grocery store, NASA driver's module, a Wasserstrom kitchen and mini-apartment. Working with Columbus businesses and interdisciplinary professionals, she developed a comprehensive assessment process. Neurological patients were tested for levels of independent functioning to determine possible changes in medication and rehabilitation. Many patients who seemed destined for nursing homes returned to their own homes instead, fully functional and able to care for themselves. Her work offered such new insights about independence thinking that *USA Today* featured her in a cover story with a several-page spread.

From 1983 until 1989, under the sponsorship of SAMC, Dr. Florance created a postgraduate residency for interdisciplinary training. Residents enrolled with backgrounds in speech-language pathology, nursing, social work, and occupational and physical therapy. Medical students and residents also participated in training experiences with children, adults and executives.

In 1982, Dr. Florance worked with Jack Tetirick, M.D., Harvard-trained Surgeon and Director of Medical Education at Grant Hospital. They implemented pilot projects as a foundation for a brainpower lab for executives. Dr. Florance developed her Brain Friendly Communication Systems for business executives to improve oral delivery, reading speed, power writing, quick recall and fluid memory.

In 1983 and 1984, Dr. Florance gave birth to Vanessa and William. They came to work with her everyday and participated in all of her programs for young children. The therapists and teachers tried new ideas on them. Because all of her therapies involved singing, dancing and acting, the kids loved to go to work with mommy. She was at the top of her game professionally, with international recognition and even an appearance on *Oprah*. Her methods had helped improve the lives of thousands of people, many of whom were children.

However, Dr. Florance's life changed drastically in 1985. On September 30th, Dr. Florance was taken to the hospital with all the hopes, worries and fears shared by every expectant mother as she looked forward to the birth of her third child. The birth did not go easily. Her son's umbilical cord was wrapped around his neck four times. Although the family was relieved when he was delivered safely and the doctor declared little Whitney to be a "perfect 10," it soon became apparent that something was terribly wrong.

Joan Mondale (left), wife of the Vice President, visits Dr. Florance and former patient Naomi Berry

From the moment she held him in her arms, Dr. Florance's motherly radar told her something was different about this child. She choked down her fears, telling herself she was over-reacting after such a stressful birth, but deep down inside her instincts were screaming at her. This beautiful little boy didn't seem to know she existed. He seemed to feel no comfort from her presence. He didn't cuddle, didn't grab her fingers, didn't respond to her touch or her voice. This was not the way it had been with either Vanessa or William. Still, the doctor had said he was perfect and Dr. Florance clung to that.

Soon after his birth, Whitney was diagnosed with severe autism, deafness and was later determined to have an I.Q. of only 46. His sensory system was so disintegrated that Dr. Florance could shout in his ear and yet he could hear nothing. His arm was once accidently pinned in the door of a truck and he seemed to feel nothing. He had uncoordinated fine and gross motor systems.

By this time in her life, Dr. Florance had received one of the highest science awards from the NIH, had been interviewed by Oprah Winfrey for her successful work on stuttering, and *USA Today* had featured her for her work with stroke patients. She was known around the world for being the best in these specialized areas. Whitney was born when she was at the top of her game, yet she had no way to reach him or help him. He completely stumped her.

Despite all the obstacles, Dr. Florance believed in her son. She saw the same visual genius in his every day behavior that she had long-observed in less pronounced ways in her therapy patients. In Whitney's case, it became apparent that his visual mechanical intelligence was rapidly developing at levels far above those of his peers.

As other experts in the field could offer no hope, Dr. Florance faced alone the dilemma of how to help Whitney become a successful member of society. As she continued to observe him, Whitney "taught" Dr. Florance how to use his visual processors to create a new brain architecture for language. By the time he was in high school, Whitney's language abilities in listening, speaking, reading and writing were well above his age level on the national tests given at school. He was an excellent athlete participating on the Division II State Championship football team, earning medals in track and lettering in wrestling. Dr. Florance credits Whitney with teaching her more than any of her prior experience or education.

After SAMC closed in 1990, Dr. Florance moved her private practice to Dublin, Ohio to open The Language Gym, containing 14 simulation labs utilizing advances in computer and video technology with special audio equipment. Since the Arts continued to be a significant component, The Language Gym included an art lab and therapy stations, computer arcade, reader's theater, writer's workshop, executive excel lab, mental workout room, parent observation room and simulation classrooms.

For the next 10 years, Dr. Florance provided services in The Language Gym for patients ranging from two years in age to geriatric adults. She served as the consultant for state agencies including the Bureau of Disability Determination and the Bureau of Vocational Rehabilitation. Once a week, she held language learning rounds in which area physicians, psychologists and other professionals discussed cases with her. The Medical Park, co-owned by Mt. Carmel Hospital, contained five pediatricians and four dentists, occupational and physical therapy services and the Mt. Carmel Hospital Nutritional Center.

Although Dr. Florance is very passionate about treating her patients, being a mom brings her even greater joy. She had always organized her practice to support the needs of her children. So when Whitney was born, she adapted her work to help find a solution for him.

William and Vanessa worked daily helping Dr. Florance train Whitney to process language, hear, and to develop motor control. Dr. Florance, Will and Vanessa entered into Whitney's world of autism to draw him out into a language-based world.

Because autism is considered a psychiatric disorder by The National Institutes of Health, Dr. Florance pursued a senior fellowship in psychiatry. Her research training involved extensive mentoring from world-class scientists and also required that she mentor psychiatric residents and medical students. For the next five years, she hired nationally recognized experts to travel to her clinic to observe her providing therapy, review her charts, interview her patients and their families, and to critique her work. Her goal was to thoroughly understand the relationship between psychiatric and communication disabilities.

In his book *Psychiatric Disease and Communication Disorder*, renowned UCLA psychiatrist Dr. Dennis Cantwell presented a large body of data indicating that many mental health problems were actually caused by under-diagnosed and mistreated communication disorders, a belief that Dr. Florance felt instinctively from the moment she learned about autism. She sent him a portfolio of information on Whitney and began a correspondence that developed into a lifelong friendship.

To help her understand the emotional and physical impact of communication disability on treatment, Dr. Florance also developed a working relationship with other experts in the field: Harvard psychiatrist Dr. John Ratey, author of *Driven to Distraction: Recognizing and Coping with Attention Deficit Disorder from Childhood through Adulthood*; NIMH expert on depression Dr. Elizabeth Weller; former Chair of the University of Michigan David Daly, Ph.D.; and Ronald Goldman, Ph.D. (author of the Goldman Fristoe Woodcock tests). These experts provided significant input into her thinking about how to re-design her practice to develop the perfect treatment program for Whitney. Prior consultants included Audrey Holland, Ph.D., author of the Communication Activities in Daily Living Test; John C. Rosenbek, Ph.D., expert on the staging treatment of motor speech disorders; Leonard La Pointe, Ph.D., University of Arizona Chair and author of the Test of Auditory Processing and Reading Processing; and Robert Marshall, Ph.D., expert on auditory processing and listening comprehension.

Even with all of these brilliant minds helping her, the prognosis for Whitney was still poor because so little was really known about his disorder. Entering into new, uncharted waters, Dr. Florance continued to pursue solutions for Whitney on her own. Whitney certainly had a very challenging course to follow, but the strength of his soul and the programs implemented by his brother, sister and mother helped him progress significantly day-by-day until he was fully mainstreamed in the school system.

In the summers of 1998 and 1999, Yale-trained professor Dr. Diana Raffman allowed Dr. Florance to use her Philosophy 101 classroom as a practice lab for a group of 20 patients who were failing in verbal classes due to communication disabilities. From this treatment program, students learned thinking skills they could use in all aspects of life. Each of these struggling students was failing because they were unsuccessfully trying to learn complex verbal material by processing it using a visual thinking system. Dr. Florance taught them how to develop verbal and bimodal thinking systems, which enabled them to achieve the highest grades in the class. Vanessa, William and Whitney all audited the class.

In August 1993, Dr. Florance designed the Brain Re-Engineering program for three struggling medical students. The success of these student physicians was remarkable and led to a collaboration with the medical school's dean, John M. Stang, M.D. This collaboration led to the Neurobehavioral Cognitive Status Exam, the Medical Student Risk Factor Analysis and the Vocational Work Simulator for Ohio State University. Dr. Florance came to name hyper-visual thinkers "Opticoders" and hyper-verbal thinkers "Lexicoders."

Because of her success with Whitney, Dr. Florance began searching for other highly visual brains with no auditory processors, which she calls "Maverick Minds." By 1999, her practice was 100% devoted to these Maverick patients.

Dr. Florance is mesmerized by the study of the creative brain and the impact that communication processing has on ingenuity. All of her current patients test statistically outside the norm in many areas of creative thinking. She hesitates to call these patients "disabled," although they clearly do qualify under the Americans with Disabilities Act as communicatively disabled. In her laboratories, she is continually amazed at the brilliance and innovative thinking these patients exhibit. Providing treatment for them is like training an Olympic athlete.

In 2001, Dr. Florance negotiated book contracts with Penguin Putnam in New York City and Germany, and Simon and Schuster in the United Kingdom. In her books, *Maverick Mind*, (www.penquinputnam.com) and *A Boy Beyond Reach* (www.simonschuster.com), she describes how she taught her own autistic son, Whitney to overcome his disabilities and become symptom-free. Now, she offers genuine hope to parents who have been told by experts that there was none.

As Whitney moved through his college years successfully, Dr. Florance decided to dramatically change her own life. She created a virtual Brain Engineering Laboratory on the Internet, complete with multimedia classrooms, worldwide video conferencing, and private website portals. The success of the virtual training tools led to consultation as an expert advisor to the Department of Education in Moscow, Minister of Education for Greece, Minister of Special Education in Cyprus and the creation of training laboratories for professionals, universities, medical schools and families all over the world. She currently operates the Brain Engineering Lab from her offices at Trump Place in New York City.

Whitney and William are now both chemical engineers and Vanessa is an attorney.

⚙ *Autism: Is There Hope?*

What if there was no cure for autism because it wasn't a *disease*? What if many autistic behaviors were actually the symptoms of another disorder that wasn't being properly diagnosed? What if traditional methods of treating autism were actually treating the *symptoms* instead of the *cause* – and making the autism worse? What if the symptoms in behavior, coping and communication were all the result of an undiagnosed inability to process and produce language? If the current scientific model doesn't include testing for such an inability, how could it ever be discovered?

Science has led to many fantastic advances over the centuries, but scientists of all ages have been known to interpret the phenomenon they see based on their current body of knowledge and experience. As a result, many discoveries have remained hidden for decades or even centuries because they didn't fit the scientific model of the time. Every once in a while, however, a researcher approaches a problem from a new and unique perspective, and the positive results then change the thinking of the entire scientific community.

The Greeks figured out mathematically that the earth had to be round, and they even calculated fairly accurately the Earth's circumference. That information was lost for centuries, however, and Columbus was called insane when he claimed the earth was not flat. Nicolas Copernicus theorized in 1543 that the earth revolved around the sun, but 67 years later Galileo still had a hard time convincing anyone that Copernicus was right. In both cases, the new scientific evidence contradicted what was "known" to be "obvious fact."

If autistic behavior truly was the symptom of some other as yet unknown disorder, would the symptoms go away by addressing the underlying cause? Many disorders and diseases are diagnosed from symptoms only. Others are diagnosed from symptoms first and then by objective testing as a second step. Autism is a symptom-based diagnosis made by observing a specific group of characteristic symptoms. Usually, mental health professionals make a diagnosis based on interviews of the child and parents and by direct observation.

The preferred practice patterns established by the American Speech-Language-Hearing Association (ASHA) recommend a parent interview, a family history and a thorough symptom analysis as the first step in evaluating a child with a language disorder. Unfortunately, many doctors and teachers often misdiagnose children. This is not entirely their fault, as their diagnosis is based on a body of knowledge that does not allow for alternative thinking, and because the same symptoms can arise from a wide variety of causes. Diagnosis is often more of an art than a science. Professionals will diagnose based on their learning and experience, which often do not include the key to understanding the true nature of many "autistic" disorders.

Autism: Is There Hope?

Throughout her many years as a classically trained scientist with wide areas of research expertise on the brain and communication disorders, Dr. Florance learned that many disorders thought to be due to permanent brain malfunction could actually be improved to a symptom-free status. Even so, she might never have developed her concept of recovery from autism if it hadn't been for the birth of her third child, Whitney.

Dr. Florance's son, Whitney

Whitney was diagnosed very early with autism and he could not utter a word until he was six years old. Experts declared him as mentally handicapped in multiple ways. Whitney did not relate to any of the people around him. It was as if he were a shell without feelings. Words had no meaning for him. In fact, his mother could shout into his ear without any kind of response, as if he were deaf.

Whitney once had his arm caught in a door, yet he seemed to feel no pain. He had no concept of anyone around him as people. He didn't know what words were. His attention span was highly erratic, as were his moods. At one minute, he would be having a temper tantrum and the next minute he would be rocking in a corner flapping his hands. His problems were so severe that doctors and educators offered little hope.

With her extensive experience training children with a variety of disorders, however, Dr. Florance discerned a pattern. Whitney had a knack of returning to places he had been to earlier. He was also always ripping apart his toys and examining their inner workings. At one point, she caught him with a knife, apparently ready to take apart his own brother to see how he worked inside. Fortunately, no one was injured, but Dr. Florance was unable to sleep at nights due to the constant supervision Whitney required. The family babysitter insisted that Whitney needed "discipline."

Dr. Florance realized, however, that Whitney did not feel hatred for his brother or want to do him injury. As bizarre as his behavior often was, there were clear patterns of behavior that did not fit the mold of a "retarded" child. Everything came together one morning when Dr. Florance arose to find the kitchen a complete disaster.

Whitney had awakened again in the middle of the night and decided he was hungry. At first, all Dr. Florance noticed was the mess of pancake syrup, milk, Cheerios and other assorted foodstuffs mixed in a large pile and strewn all over the kitchen floor. How Whitney even managed to reach some of the items in the supposedly "child proof" kitchen was mystery enough, but everything became crystal clear when Dr. Florance looked in the oven.

Sitting in the (fortunately unlit) oven was a bowl. In the bowl were the contents of an empty cake mix box, some water, and *three unbroken eggs*. It was the three eggs that told the story. They were unbroken – just like the pictures on the box of cake mix!

Whitney was *problem-solving!* He was *thinking!* He had seen the picture on the box and recreated it exactly, but when nothing happened after that, when it didn't turned out like he planned, when there was no *cake*, he became frustrated and angry and simply made his own "breakfast" all over the floor.

That was the moment that Dr. Florance realized her instincts so many years ago about autism had to be correct. Whitney did not have a psychiatric or mental health problem, he had a communication problem. Whitney clearly had a mind capable of reason, determination, problem-solving and goal-achieving – but in a visual manner. What he lacked was a language to communicate his desires to the outside world. He was thinking in *pictures*, not words!

This is something that would have been missed by any parent without extensive research knowledge. No casual researcher interviewing the child or parents would have been able to interpret this behavior from occasional observation or questionnaires. You had to *be there* to see these incidents to realize that this was no mentally handicapped boy. Whitney seemed to be accessing his visual memory and had a highly visual, mechanical way of thinking.

Dr. Florance also began noticing patterns in Whitney's behavior that seemed to mirror those of patients in her other research—research that would seem to have no connection to autism in the traditional sense. These included stutterers, preschool children who were speech and language impaired, and brain-damaged hospital patients. She began to theorize the possibility that some of these methods or a combination of them might be able to help her son. For Whitney's sake, that possibility had to become a reality.

Dr. Florance had developed therapies that produced dramatic improvement before. The average child admitted to the Head Start program started out at a level two years behind the norm, yet they were brought up to normal performance after only 20 to 25 sessions. These children started out with difficulties listening, reading, writing and speaking, yet many became able to perform well above the normal range.

Traditional stuttering treatment methods had used negative reinforcement to stop the pattern of stuttering. Rather than teach stutterers what not to do, Dr. Florance's approach was to replace the stuttering patterns with positive, stutter-free behaviors. Although it was revolutionary at the time, the method is now taught in universities internationally.

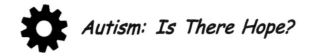 *Autism: Is There Hope?*

Dr. Florance's articles on stroke patient aphasia and apraxia are recommended by the ASHA as Best Practices. She provided guidance for rehabilitation teams working with brain injury and stroke patients. Her work was featured on the front page of *USA Today* and honored by many medically-based research facilities.

In all of these cases, Dr. Florance had found ways to help those whom others had deemed without hope. There had to be a way to help her son as well. She was determined to find it and she did, but the road was far from easy.

Whitney's First Two Years

Could it be that the trauma of Whitney's birth could have affected him somehow? Could the umbilical cord being wrapped around his neck have cut of the blood to his developing brain in a way that might have affected its development? It may be that Whitney suffered blood loss to the brain during this time period, which in addition to the stress of a difficult birth, may have affected him in a manner similar to stroke victims. There is no way to know for certain, but at the time, Dr. Florance simply *felt* something was different about her son. As Whitney grew, the problems became indisputable.

Whitney's brother William and sister Vanessa, neither of whom were much older than him, seemed to be able to understand and interpret Whitney better than the adults, although there was still a big gap in understanding the odd behaviors and random outbursts that occurred for apparently no reason. Whitney's mom brought him to the office where he could watch the art, drama, and occupational and speech therapists engage the other children. She also set him on a routine schedule that included a set time for playing in the sandbox, taking a bath, etc. She hoped that, even though he seemed to exhibit no awareness, somewhere inside himself he might begin to recognize and understand a pattern to his life.

As he continued to grow, however, Dr. Florance's heart sank as she witnessed the first signs of perseveration in her son. Perseveration is a random, uncontrollable repetition of a word, phrase or gesture for no apparent reason. It usually indicates a brain injury or a serious organic disorder. She watched as Whitney mechanically unraveled a roll of toilet paper in the bathroom. Now this is something that all kids do and it can be funny or annoying to watch, but the *way* he was doing it terrified her. He was not "playing" with the roll; he was like a robot. She feared that this could be an early indication of more severe disorders. Sadly, it was.

Whitney at Age Two

By the time he was two, professionals had diagnosed Whitney with a multitude of disorders, including mental retardation and deafness. He rated only a 46 on the IQ test. Remembering how her students felt who were sent to "stupid class" for dance lessons, Dr. Florance was determined to include Whitney in as much of her daily activity as possible. It was about this age when Dr. Florance noticed Whitney was attracted to mechanical, cause-and-effect type toys, like the Jack-in-the-box.

Despite the fact that he was obviously severely handicapped, Whitney was exhibiting a tremendous amount of curiosity. Each positive discovery, however, was often followed by a significant, inexplicable setback. One night, while staying at a hotel, Dr. Florance was awakened in the middle of the night by the police. Whitney had pulled apart the entertainment center in the room, unlocked the door to the hallway, and found his way down the elevator to the hotel kitchen. He had figured out how to open the refrigerator, fed himself, took off all his clothes, and fell asleep. Most parents would be appalled at this behavior, but Dr. Florance was encouraged. She didn't see this as bad behavior, but recognized the complex series of cognitive skills and decision-making (executive planning, sequencing, logic reasoning and hypothesis testing) it had taken for Whitney to accomplish all this. For a child who was supposed to have an IQ of only 46, this should have been impossible. He had exhibited rational thought and awareness that was well beyond the average two-year-old.

Whitney at Three

By age three, Whitney's fits had become disturbing. For no apparent reason and without any provocation, he would throw a tantrum that turned his face beet red, yet there were no tears or sounds of crying. Often he would throw himself to the ground, thrashing, biting, kicking or banging his head. Holding him close did not seem to comfort him. Soothing words did not calm him. The only option was to try to keep him from hurting himself or others until he tired himself out and went back to his normal, unresponsive self or fell asleep.

Concerned about his ability to socialize, Dr. Florance entered Whitney into a pre-school class for two-year-olds. She also began to alter the focus of her private practice towards highly visual patients with communication problems, in order to devote as much time as possible to attacking the mystery behind Whitney's brain problems.

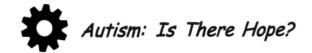

It was at this age that Whitney's pediatrician informed Dr. Florance that he believed Whitney was autistic and required professional help. This would mean separating Whitney from his family and placing him largely in isolation. Despite her pediatrician's recommendations, Florance believed this would only worsen Whitney's condition. To place Whitney with other seriously disabled children would eliminate any chance that he could learn normal behavior. How could he learn "normal" behavior if he was surrounded only by children who exhibited the same symptoms? How could this do anything but reinforce those symptoms? She decided to give him as much of a mainstream education as possible.

Despite her determination and optimism, the school board did not agree.

Whitney at Four

Forced to enroll Whitney in a specialized school, Dr. Florance moved her entire family to Dublin, Ohio so Whitney could attend a promising autism pre-school for children with severe developmental delays. Even among other children with severe development issues, however, Whitney was seen as the worst student by the teachers. They placed him in the "unteachable" program. When they tried to talk to him, he would bang his head and bite people and rip things up. The same thing happened if the fire alarm went off. He even would pull down his pants and pee on anyone who got too close when he didn't want them to. Most parents would be appalled and ashamed if their child behaved this way, and they would have taken the teachers' advice that there was nothing they could do. Most kids, though, don't have brain doctors for a mom.

Again, what seemed like problem behavior actually encouraged Whitney's mom. She saw a pattern that indicated Whitney was hearing too much and then not enough. The response by the teachers to negative behavior was to *talk* to Whitney or *scold* him. This was like beating him over the head with words and he couldn't handle it. They were only providing more of the same stimuli that he was negatively responding to in the first place. The fact that he peed on people meant he was communicating in the only way he knew how. The message was, "Stay away!" (and it was pretty effective).

Because Dr. Florance was an internationally recognized brain doctor, the school couldn't really prevent her from showing up every day as a self-appointed "parent volunteer assistant." Besides, they'd rather have her deal with his tantrums than have to deal with Whitney themselves. They couldn't be blamed (or sued) if anything went wrong.

Using the techniques she had first outlined in her Master's thesis, Dr. Florance wrote little operas for the children. She also brought her guitar and interacted with the kids in song.

Although he still had a long way to go, by the end of the year, Whitney actually began showing signs of improvement.

Whitney at Five

People do not always operate with the most noble of motives. The reaction of school officials was to ban Whitney. Why? Parents were coming in asking the school officials why Whitney seemed to be making much more improvement than their children were.

At end of the year, the head of the program said Whitney couldn't stay. Dr. Florance asked if he could repeat the year as other children had been allowed to do. The first excuse was, "Anyone born on or after September 30th can't be in this program." This seemed more than a little coincidental since Whitney had been born precisely on September 30th. With only four children in the program, Whitney would magically be the only one excluded.

Dr. Florance decided to enroll Whitney in another school—a new school—in the same district that was opening up very near her home. The guidance counselor that Dr. Florance liked and respected was being sent to work at that school, so this would have been ideal. That's when the ruling was announced that anyone living on the 4500 block of Harriet Road couldn't be in *that* school. This just happened to coincide with Dr. Florance's address—and only her address. Having a somewhat large piece of property that bordered two streets, a friend at the post office changed address so the prohibition would no longer apply. Almost predictably, the program officials sent out another clarification that they had made a "mistake" in the original notice, no one living on the street of Dr. Florance's new address would be allowed.

Dr. Florance entered Whitney in yet another school and was disappointed when the staff labeled him "multi-handicapped." She brushed it off, however. She was used to this by now. She couldn't really blame them. How could she, when she knew that she herself was the first person ever to develop this kind of research with this kind of progress? Besides, if he had not been diagnosed in this manner, he would not have been allowed to go to this school, due to governmental guidelines.

Despite her resistance to Whitney being "warehoused" with dysfunctional children (many of whom were on strong medication), it turned out to be a blessing in disguise. Because so much less was expected of these students, the classroom was less restrictive and therefore allowed more flexibility – the kind of flexibility that would enable Dr. Florance to try new methods of teaching her son. She worked with Whitney's new classroom teacher, Mrs. Jones,

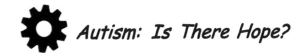

to implement a pre-reading program to teach Whitney the concept of words much like Anne Sullivan taught Helen Keller through finger spelling. Anne Sullivan had been a hero of Dr. Florance's and her work seemed applicable here.

Anne Sullivan herself had become blind at the age of 3 due to trachoma, a ravaging bacterial infection of the eyes. She went to the prestigious Perkins School for the Blind in Watertown, Massachusetts where, as part of her studies, she learned a method of sign language for blind people that was developed by Spanish monks in the middle ages. Pressing upon specific areas of the left or right hand indicated letters that allowed communication with deaf and blind people. After a multitude of surgeries, she had much of her sight restored, so Sullivan was sent to teach Helen Keller how to communicate using this sign language alphabet. It worked so well that Helen actually learned to talk, became a prolific writer, and the two became inseparable friends for life.

Dr. Florance knew an "alphabet glove" would be of no use to Whitney, since he often did not respond to physical stimuli. However, the same kind of "out of the box" thinking might lead to a similar unconventional language – one based on *visual* cues and ideas. Realizing that Whitney was in fact aware of his surroundings and family, and was able to recall things he had seen (he didn't make his way down an elevator and straight to the kitchen of a strange hotel by accident), Dr. Florance developed a new "game" to play. She used labels from various household items and corporate logos of places where Whitney liked to go. She placed these on the floor and played word games with her other children in front of Whitney. She made this part of a routine she was building for her son, whether he seemed to be interested or not.

One day, Whitney handed Dr. Florance a flashcard with a fast food chain logo on it—it was the place where he loved to go and eat French fries. With tears in her eyes, she started shouting for joy. Whitney had *communicated* to her! He had *asked* for something! Needless to say, she rushed him right out the door and got him the French fries he wanted. He did not throw a fit on this outing. He had communicated a need and received what he wanted. This was in every sense a breakthrough.

By forcing Whitney to relocate to a different school designed to manage children with severe disorders, Whitney's school administration was clearly making a statement: they did not believe he had made any improvement. Dr. Florance had seen improvement, but if Whitney was going to be accepted into a mainstream first-grade program, he would need to improve much more. He would have to be able to understand spoken directions and he would have to be able to *read*. He was now making vocal sounds but they were gibberish with no clear pattern. She had to design a way to teach Whitney to read using only his visual ability. Mrs. Jones was highly supportive of Dr. Florance's efforts and even helped improve upon them.

Then one day, the unthinkable happened.

Whitney at Six

One Halloween day, after playing guitar and singing in his class, a strange little voice spoke up. It was a voice no one had ever heard before. The voice called out, "Dr. Florance!" Neither she nor Mrs. Jones could tell who had called her name. Whitney came up to his mom and gave her a big hug. "Dr. Florance!" he called again.

It was Whitney! When she bent down to see what her son wanted, he handed her a gummy worm, then popped one of his own into his mouth smiling. When they both got over the shock and excitement, Mrs. Jones asked, "Why didn't he call you 'mom' or 'momma'?" Dr. Florance started to ponder this, then stopped, thinking instead to herself, "Who cares! He spoke! And he recognized me!" It didn't matter *what* he called her, he had *spoken!* Besides, since everyone at all his schools had always called her Dr. Florance, it really wasn't that surprising. Suddenly, Dr. Florance knew how Annie Sullivan must have felt all those decades ago when Helen Keller uttered her childhood word for water: wah-wah. Only Helen wasn't Annie's true, flesh and blood child.

This was an amazing breakthrough on so many other levels as well. Whitney, the newborn baby who never cuddled or responded to touch, had initiated a hug! He also had exhibited social skills. By offering her one of his gummy worms, he was *sharing*. She was no longer just a recurring picture in his world – she had become a *person* to him. From then on, he would actually want to hold his mother's hand and he began vocalizing attempts at verbal communication.

After all her hard work and perseverance, operating as much on instinct and gut-level intuition as on her scientific training, Dr. Florance finally had objective evidence that her methods were working. More importantly, she had confirmation that Whitney did indeed recognize and connect with her as his mother. It was like a light bulb had been turned on in a previously dark room. Whitney began to develop much more of a relationship with his mother and the world around him.

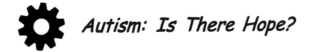 *Autism: Is There Hope?*

Preparing Whitney for First Grade

Whitney had made a major breakthrough, but he still had a long way to go. Even though he could say his mother's name, he mostly spoke gibberish. The next goal was to get him to understand that words have meaning so he could express his thoughts using spoken language. What most children begin to learn from the moment they're born by absorbing the sounds around them, Whitney was only now beginning to learn. Whitney's mom began a new program with the goal of teaching him about 25 new words a week. He began to read, not like a normal six-year-old, but by recognizing groups of words.

Despite these successes, Dr. Florance dreaded meeting with school officials about Whitney's plans for first grade, since most of the skills considered necessary for first grade were still missing. True, he was well behind other children his age who had developed "normally," but his progress compared to where he was even a year prior was off the chart with a strong likelihood that he would continue to improve exponentially.

Now that Whitney had opened up, his mom began to see even more clearly than ever that Whitney was fascinated with visual tasks. His model building, his high visual scores and his fascination with staring at things for hours on end were all linked. She began to suspect she was discovering a new syndrome that no one had ever heard of. One that (at least in Whitney's case) presented symptoms identical to autism, but which could be corrected with the right kind of therapy. If Whitney had been so often labeled "unteachable," how many other children might also benefit from the discoveries she was making? How many parents were told there was no hope, where hope might well exist?

They expanded on the pictures and logos game. They couldn't teach Whitney to read in the normal manner, where children learn the alphabet and associate sounds with each letter in order to group the sounds into words. He was a visual thinker, so he needed to learn to read visually. Dr. Florance taught him to read entire words by association. She added written words to the picture/logo cards she had created, then gradually shifted to word-only cards.

Dr. Florance also built stories around Whitney's experiences to give the words practical meaning. That winter, there was a big snowfall and kids everywhere were outside busy having snowball fights and building snowmen. William and Vanessa took their brother outside to build a snowman that had a red hat, a carrot nose, and candy for eyes. A local news van was driving by and took some video. Sure enough, that night on the news, part of the snowfall coverage included the Florance children grinning next to their snowman. Whitney saw himself on TV and got very excited.

The whole family used the word cards to tell this story to Whitney, hoping that he might recognize at least one or two of the words. There was no way to know if this was really getting through to him, however. One day, William and Vanessa shouted, "Hooray!" from the living room. When their mother ran in to see what was up, they excitedly proclaimed, "He did it! Whitney 'wrote' the story!" Sure enough, the words on the table had been laid out in the following order: SNOWMAN RED HAT CARROT NOSE CANDY EYES.

They say that if a million monkeys type at a million typewriters, they will eventually write all the works of Shakespeare, but that is categorically false. It takes rational thought to put words in a particular order. A million monkeys at a million typewriters for a million years might type out disconnected words, but there is an infinite combination of gibberish and only one combination that can come from rational thought. Whitney had not been randomly putting words together for no reason, he had remembered the pattern that told the story and was able to recreate it. He knew what the story was about and had recreated it to share with his family. By definition, this was communication.

All we do when we communicate is repeat phrases with assorted variations to convey a meaning. We say, "Good Morning." "Have a good morning." "Did you have a good morning?" If Whitney could recognize words in a certain order that conveyed meaning, then he might be able to read words in a particular order on a page and understand their meaning. If he could be taught to recognize those words and put them in order to convey meaning, then he would, by definition, be able to communicate.

Despite all the progress Whitney had made and the improved behavior he was exhibiting, the school system only saw Whitney for what he *couldn't* do, rather than what he could do. They still insisted on tests that required him to write answers and he still didn't have the fine motor control over a pencil that would allow him to do that. Mrs. Jones went to bat for Whitney, but although they did admit he had made improvement (a shocking breakthrough in itself), they were not ready to mainstream him just yet. He was assigned to a first grade program for highly functioning autistic children. He would have four classmates and two teachers. Despite the heartbreak, this was again probably the best thing for Whitney.

American schools are not designed to tailor teaching methods toward the needs of individual students, they are designed to teach a generally acceptable grade level of material and it is up to the students to adapt and learn. Rather than be lost in a system that didn't understand him and made no deviations from the teaching norm, he would get the attention he needed. In such a small class, Whitney would be able to continue building his word bank, using the program his mother had devised for him.

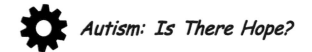

Still, the mother in Dr. Florance was angry. She felt she had poured her heart and soul into getting Whitney ready for first grade, only to be knocked down again. Too little, too late. Yet, on the last day of school, instead of the fights and battles associated with getting him out of the car and into the school that were so common in the beginning, Whitney, got out of the car and walked straight to class all by himself. As he approached the door to his classroom, he waved at some of the other students. Then, he turned around and yelled to Dr. Florance, "I wuuuuv ooooou, Mom!" What would be taken for granted with any other child, grabbed her heart a thousand times over. No, Whitney would not be going to a "mainstream" first grade next year, but this was no time to give up. Too much had been gained to quit now.

That summer, Whitney made great progress but there were some setbacks. If he was over-stimulated in a public forum, he still might run off and need to be calmed down. He could repeat stories with his words and his brother and sister had taught him "charades," so he was acting out roles in little plays his family had devised, but he wasn't really creating anything on his own. It was Vanessa, the veteran first grader, who suggested they use theatre to teach Whitney how to tell a story. She explained that in first grade, the kids had to tell a story with a beginning, middle and an end – something Whitney still couldn't do. They got a bunch of costumes and old clothes from Whitney's grandmother to use in their own home "theatre" and Vanessa took over this part of Whitney's training.

First Grade

Although it wasn't a fully mainstreamed class, Whitney's first grade wasn't totally segregated, either. Although Dr. Florance reluctantly accepted the "autistic" label the school placed on Whitney so he could receive the attention he needed, she never accepted the prognosis. Like so many other parents, she was told yet again there was no treatment and no hope. The school evaluators could never know the extent of progress Whitney had made, and Dr. Florance had no definitive study to present to try and change their minds – yet. It was more important to focus on Whitney and develop his treatment programs than to get into needless arguments with school officials. Although he still couldn't hear normally and could barely speak, Whitney's mom was more determined than ever to get Whitney fully mainstreamed into school. The progress he had made showed her it *was* possible.

Despite Whitney's promotion from "unteachable" to the autistic class, Dr. Florance approached the first school day with fear and trepidation. She worried that the break in routine would cause a setback. Whitney had traditionally had a hard time making friends and adapting to new environments. Her fears vanished, however, when she pulled up to the school to see the principal, Mr. Niemie, standing outside playing a guitar and singing to all the kids that were arriving. She had no problem getting Whitney out of the car to see what all the fun was about.

Mr. Niemie knew exactly who Whitney was and everything about him. He put the guitar down, came straight to Whitney, lifted him high into the air and welcomed him. Things seemed to fall apart, however, when they reached Whitney's classroom.

The room was very small and barren. As soon as Whitney saw it, he started waving his arms and tried to leave. The students were classically autistic, and Dr. Florance worried that Whitney might return to some of his old autistic behaviors by being around them all day. Sadly, she was right. Whitney began occasionally exhibiting some of his old behaviors not long after school started. Dr. Florance pleaded with Mr. Niemie to let Whitney move into the mainstream first grade.

Mr. Niemie actually understood what Dr. Florance was saying, but he also understood the difficulty. There were bureaucratic regulations against them, and there were personal issues with some of the teachers who didn't like their competency to teach Whitney questioned. Mr. Niemie masterfully handled all the objections and by the time Whitney turned seven on September 30th, Mr. Niemie had reached a compromise that allowed Whitney to spend most of the day in the regular 1st grade class. He even told the teachers that if Whitney had any kind of disruptive episode, he would personally take Whitney into his office and take care of him until he calmed down. He was willing to put his own job on the line against people who thought Dr. Florance was overly optimistic, blind to reality, or just plain crazy.

In October, Dr. Florance went to Whitney's first parent-teacher conference. She expected the worst and didn't know what to think when the first grade teacher broke down in tears. She said that Whitney had adapted beyond all expectations. He still needed help with math, since he could count to 28 (with a lot of coaching) but he could read the kids' names on folders. His handwriting was atrocious but he was able to write a full story. The other kids had accepted him.

"This is a miracle!" she said finally. "Whitney is a miracle. Thank you for allowing me to be part of this."

There were, of course, difficulties. One of the teachers, who had been against Whitney and his mother from the start, could see only the most negative aspects of the situation and noted them in her reports. Whitney was well below average in many respects compared to other first graders, but considering he wasn't even supposed to be in first grade according to the "experts" who wanted him in the autistic class, even "below average" was a dramatic improvement. Many of the skills he had never had before were evaluated to be "average." By the end of the year, he was upgraded to "Learning Disabled."

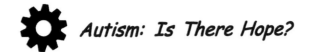 *Autism: Is There Hope?*

Most parents wouldn't cheer about their child being branded as LD, but for Dr. Florance, it meant her hard work was paying off. If Whitney's learning curve continued to spiral upward, he might actually make it into MIT one day as Dr. Florance had hoped. Mr. Niemie was committed to doing everything in his power to help that along.

During the summer between first and second grades Whitney improved dramatically. Dr. Florance continued to work with him, building a safety net of support around him so he could continue to improve. The fact that – for the first time – he was allowed to return to the same school meant minimal change in the routine he had become used to. The following school year went well for him.

Second Grade

Whitney continued to improve and his second grade teacher was happy to have Dr. Florance show her how to best help her son. She even invited Dr. Florance to lead a writing workshop. At first only a few kids signed up (including Whitney), but soon the whole class wanted to join. Dr. Florance made it fun to learn and rewarded each of them with praise and stickers for a job well done.

Then she received a certified letter from the American Speech-Language-Hearing Association stating they had received complaints from several school psychologists. One of the psychologists had actually asked Dr. Florance in the past why she thought visual processing had anything to do with language. Dr. Florance responded with a lengthy response that both visual and auditory processing are the primary neurological systems necessary to process language through listening, speaking, reading and writing. A blind person might be able to speak, but he or she would not be able to read normal written text, and written language is still language. Dr. Florance had not heard from this psychologist again, but obviously, along with others, the ASHA had.

The charges were serious. If she did not respond, the ASHA could pull her license as a speech and language therapist. She was provided with the "evidence" presented against her, which was composed of numerous personal attacks and the allegation that she was misrepresenting herself as a "psychologist" who was providing mental health services. Part of the evidence came from a television news video where the reporter (*after* the interview) referred to Dr. Florance as a psychologist, although she never had identified herself as one. The reporter later admitted he had just assumed that her Ph.D. degree meant she was a psychologist.

In yet another bizarre twist of ironic fate, what appeared to be a disaster turned out to aligned as the most respected doctors in the field arranged to investigate Dr. Florance's work a be the best thing possible. The ASHA assigned a team of experts to study Dr. Florance's methods, and she was allowed to invite other experts in the field who were already familiar with her work to attend as well. After studying others for decades, now Dr. Florance was under the microscope. She was to be studied and evaluated and for Whitney's sake, as well as her own, she had to prevail. Dr. Cantwell himself, who had received a lifetime achievement award from the American Psychiatric Association (so his credentials and objectivity were beyond question) responded to a letter sent by Dr. Florance and agreed to be one of the observers. The stars The stars aligned as the most respected doctors in the field arranged to investigate Dr. Florance's work and Whitney's progress.

The process took an entire year and in the end, not only did the ASHA clear Dr. Florance, but its members were fascinated by her research and sent an additional list of questions for clarification to further their understanding. There was no denying that Whitney, the boy the school board had labeled as "unteachable," was now able to read and write and socialize, nor that many of Dr. Florance's other patients had also shown marked improvement, nor that her research was sound. Dr. Florance actually received letters of apology from the ASHA and State Board of Speech Pathology, both of which cleared her completely.

Third Grade

At the start of Whitney's third grade year, Mr. Niemie began an experimental program combining children from the third and fourth grades. The idea was that children who excelled at a subject like math could learn with the older kids, while those who had a harder time in a given subject could learn at their own pace without judgment. This meant a larger class size of around 50 children, however, and Dr. Florance – who had been pushing to accelerate Whitney's progress for years – suddenly became reluctant, fearing this situation was too different and might be pushing him too fast, too soon. There were to be only two teachers and *no* mother assistants. Mr. Niemie asked her to let Whitney give it a try for six weeks.

Dr. Florance was correct. The change was too much for Whitney to handle, and he temporarily relapsed into some of his old behaviors. He spoke less and had little interaction with his classmates. He was at least able by this time to recognize his own frustration level and was usually able to remove himself from a situation before it developed into a full-blown episode. Still, he was often withdrawn when he failed to comply with some request he didn't understand.

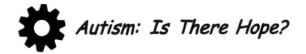

After two weeks, Whitney's teachers called Dr. Florance in for a meeting and explained he could not continue in their class. When asked, "Why not?" they responded that Whitney was disobedient.

By this time, Dr. Florance knew that Whitney was never willfully disobedient. If he did not comply, it was because he didn't understand the request. When Dr. Florance asked for an example, the teachers explained that Whitney was told to read two chapters on the Civil War. Twenty minutes later, the class was told to put the books away and take out their math books. When he was personally told to stop reading, he acted as if he didn't hear them.

Dr. Florance explained that the truth was, he probably *didn't* hear them. Whitney was a visual thinker, and for years he seemed unable to hear at all because the visual images dominated his brain. He had learned to read whole words by associating them with pictures. That meant that when he read about something like the Civil War, his mind was so filled with images that the overactive visual processing in his brain would actually block out his ability to hear.

Reading, after all, is a visual skill, and Whitney had only recently emerged from a silent world where visual images had literally dominated his life. He had to put the words into order visually to be able to completely understand them. Just as he used to stare at his own face in the mirror or at some other object for hours, mentally taking it apart and examining it from every angle, he was doing the same thing with his reading. He was not reading slowly because he wasn't sure of the words, he was reading visually at the speed of light computing all of the myriads of visual possibilities. Like a supercomputer working on an astrophysics equation, despite the speed of the processor, the requested information can require hours of processing.

As Whitney later explained, "If she wants me to learn about the Civil War, why does she interrupt me when I am halfway understanding something and tell me to do something else? I will forget what I have read and have to read it over again." It is very difficult to argue against that kind of logic. Not bad for a kid who's IQ was supposed to be 46.

Dr. Florance explained that Whitney was not trying to be disrespectful, and politely suggested they really couldn't blame Whitney for being unclear about the directions they had given him. She suggested the next time they should write a short instruction on a sticky note and place it on his desk. That way, he would visually see and understand the instructions and he would comply. Whitney eventually came to understand that if they said to read two chapters, what they really *meant* was, "Read two chapters if you can, or read as much of the two chapters as possible until we say stop."

Mr. Niemie, however, was also correct. By the time the sixth week was over, Whitney had settled into his new routine, and the rest of the school year went smoothly. Once the rules in the classroom were made clear, Whitney complied beautifully. The two teachers were open to learning about how to reach Whitney and they came to greatly appreciate him. When Dr. Florance's book, *Maverick Mind* was released, they came to a book signing to give Whitney a hug.

Fourth Grade

Dr. Florance was now confident that teaching Whitney language and fixing his communication problem was eliminating the psychiatric symptoms associated with autism. She and her other children would again be amazed by Whitney's progress when he says, "I just wish we could all sit down and talk together." Up until that time, he had never made a point of directly sharing his feelings.

As a result, they began family discussion meetings, where everyone could share something in their lives. Differences in communication styles between them emerged, which enabled a greater understanding all the way around. Dr. Florance, for example, would verbalize around her feelings or story, thinking out loud as she went. Whitney once complained, "Why don't you just get to the point?" Many people use speaking as a social interchange, talking and listening. Visual thinkers like Whitney saw language as a tool to get something done. In fact, it was observed that Whitney spoke English as though it were a second language, which in many ways, it was. He was often oblivious to nuance or propriety in his speaking.

The family discussions helped broaden Whitney's awareness, communication skills, and helped the entire family bond. The little boy who had been silent for so long now had a lot to say and he was being listened to. He also was able to observe and absorb how other people used communication – whether it annoyed him at times or not.

Fifth Grade

Fifth Grade brought about another tough transition for Whitney. He had to relocate to a different school without all of the supports created for him over the previous three years. Mr. Niemie was being transferred to another school and wrote a letter to the school board recommending that Whitney join him, but they insisted Whitney had to attend a school within the district he was zoned for.

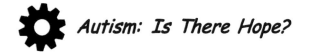

It turned out that Whitney's teacher at the local school was the same one he had when he was four years old. She was amazed that Whitney had progressed enough to be in her 5th grade class and she was highly supportive. She was thrilled to see Whitney again, but oddly enough, Whitney had no memory of her at all.

In fact, Whitney had no memory of his life before age 7. It was as if memory was somehow linked to the ability to verbally communicate. This seems to be the case, for visual images are by their very nature received in a steady stream. Words and language are the context we use to create associations, so words seem to provide the structure necessary to categorize and retain information. The left temporal brain lobe not only handles verbal processing, but also speech, comprehension and verbal memory.

You may remember a favorite scene from a movie if someone mentions the title of the movie, or asks about your favorite romantic scene, or a particular actor—all of these provide a context to *categorize* the same visual image. With no context whatsoever, the scenes may simply replay over and over in the mind (as when Whitney was able to remember how to get down to the hotel kitchen) but eventually they are replaced with new streaming images. Common images of a restaurant that has your favorite French fries might be remembered because they are linked to a visceral context: being hungry or the desire for French fries. Otherwise, if there is no context, the images may never be retrieved. When the movie stops playing, it is gone. Whatever the reason, Whitney's memory of his life only began when he started speaking.

The year did not start out well. Whitney needed routine to help him understand his surroundings. The new school seemed chaotic to him and he struggled. A new game plan was created to pair Whitney up with a study buddy, a recess partner and a lunch partner. This would enable him to develop a few closer relationships to build his social skills, and also give him help getting where he needed to go and back. To prevent Whitney from being singled out, the teacher made this a policy for the entire class. It turned out that all the kids liked the idea. Whitney continued to learn and improve.

That year, the 5th graders participated in a Drug Abuse Resistance Education (DARE) program sponsored by the local police. There was a contest for kids to come up with anti-drug messages. Whitney wrote and presented a one-man play, complete with costumes, comedic voices and facial expressions. Surprisingly, he came in third. None of the judges knew anything about his history of disabilities. Whitney's handwriting skills were still far below the norm, but he was improving rapidly.

Sixth Grade

Although Dr. Florance had high hopes for her son's sixth grade year, she was also concerned about him attending yet another new school. Whitney's stability depended greatly on routine, and this would be the first year Whitney would have to change classrooms after each period. Whitney's older brother would be attending the school as well, but he would not be in the same classes to help Whitney along. Dr. Florance was also worried about how the other children would react to Whitney. Out of 1,000 children, only Whitney and two others were in special education classes.

Sure enough, there were more issues and challenges. Whitney faced the ugliness of discrimination for the first time as some of the kids teased him for being a "retard." Although this deeply hurt the highly sensitive boy, it also motivated him. He was more determined than ever to shed his remaining disabilities. He spoke to his principal who set up a highly unusual meeting where Whitney could plead his case to the teachers involved.

Whitney spoke on his own behalf, explaining that he was getting A's in his mainstream classes: History, Science and Art. He was confident that he could do well in English and Math as well if given the chance. The teachers were not convinced. They pointed out that he was still hard to understand at times and his handwriting was poor. They felt he clearly needed the special ed classes. The principal, however, gave

Whitney a partial victory. Once he suggested that Whitney could be moved to honors math but remain in special ed English and homeroom, the rest of the teachers agreed.

Seventh and Eighth Grades

Whitney struggled again as he began yet another new school. Dr. Florance sent him to a private academy where, for the first time, there were no special education classes. For his part, Whitney refused to let Dr. Florance help out at his school. This was life-changing for Dr. Florance, who had always been around, developing and refining Whitney's therapy, but she understood completely. Whitney was becoming his own man. He wanted to make it on his own and he had become confident enough in himself to know he could do it. Dr. Florance also understood that no boy at that age wanted his mommy hanging around the school all the time. He had been teased mercilessly at his last school for being a "retard," she couldn't let the kids at this school think he was a "momma's boy."

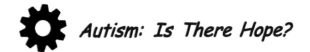 *Autism: Is There Hope?*

Despite her worries, Dr. Florance backed off (although she still was always willing to help at home if asked). In these two years, Whitney worked hard at school and with his family at home to get his reading and writing up to high school levels. He was also developing new a connection to his feelings.

Whitney had once told his mother that he had no feelings. Dr. Florance knew that wasn't true. Whitney felt very upset when the kids teased him. He felt determined to do something about it. He felt frustrated when he couldn't figure out what the teachers wanted him to do. Still, he didn't connect to his feelings in the same way that other people do, so it appeared to him that he didn't even have feelings—certainly not what other people called or experienced as feelings.

This emotional disconnect turned out to be common in visual thinkers. It isn't that they don't have feelings, but the feelings or emotions are triggered in a different manner. When two girls saw the movie *Titanic*, they discussed the romantic and tragic scenes afterward, but they could find no agreement. One of them had emotions that were triggered by the visual images, and the other's emotions were triggered by the verbal aspects of the story. Other highly visual thinkers do not seem to have the same range of emotions as verbal thinkers.

This may be explained by the intense frustration highly visual thinkers feel while growing up. When Whitney was unable to communicate, he would throw silent fits and rages. Cleary, he was experiencing very strong emotions. Other Mavericks say they have few emotions. One explained she had only two: anger and happiness (and she was angry 90% of the time).

The frustration and anger encountered so often in life may simply overwhelm all other emotions. How can one know the subtleties and nuances of emotions like annoyance or sadness if frustration and anger are constantly raging? Other emotions are closely linked to those around us, and we have seen how those with communication impairments are less able (or unable) to connect to the people around them. How can you like someone, or feel love, or feel sadness at someone else's loss if you have no connection to people? How can you worry about someone if they are only a visual image in your silent world? How can you put words to your feelings if you have no words to use?

As with memory, language seems to be the key to understanding and expressing one's own feelings and emotions. As language grows, so do the feelings, or at least the expression of them. At the very least, the greater the facility of language, the better one is able to understand one's own feelings and explore them. Language clearly can help define and even enhance emotions.

Consider the following poem:
> Roses are red.
> Violets are blue.
> Sugar is sweet.
> And so are you.
> *--Anonymous*

Compare that with the following:

> How do I love thee? Let me count the ways.
> I love thee to the depth and breadth and height
> My soul can reach, when feeling out of sight
> For the ends of being and ideal grace.
> I love thee to the level of every day's
> Most quiet need, by sun and candle-light.
> I love thee freely, as men strive for right.
> I love thee purely, as they turn from praise.
> I love thee with the passion put to use
> In my old griefs, and with my childhood's faith.
> I love thee with a love I seemed to lose
> With my lost saints. I love thee with the breath,
> Smiles, tears, of all my life; and, if God choose,
> I shall but love thee better after death.
> *--Elizabeth Barrett Browning, Sonnet 43*

Both poems speak of love, but only the expanded use of verbal language can conjure up such depth of emotion. A Maverick like Whitney, who came so late in life to language, grew up with emotions that were not defined by language – and therefore were not understood. Just as his memories had no context for organization and retrieval, the same was true for his emotions. He had learned language visually, apart from the normal associations we all make learning to speak as we grow, including the association with his own emotions.

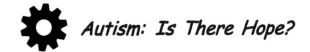

When we see our mother smiling and saying, "Mommy loves you!" there is a wide range of context involved. A baby feels good when tickled, when it hears its mother's voice, sees her smile, and it all gets associated with the words, "Mommy" and "love." Without language, the emotions get lost in history along with the images. Words are later understood merely by definition, with no internal context. The association with feelings and true *meaning* must be built after the language skills are developed, rather than simultaneously as in normal development. That is one reason why such a large part of Whitney's continued development required social interaction with others.

Whitney Makes It to High School

As in every other year, Whitney had a tough transition to his new environment, but again, he pulled through. In the 9th grade, after many years of occupational and physical therapy, Whitney was finally mainstreamed in his classes – and in a prominent college prep Catholic high school, no less. He made good grades without any accommodations or special services, and even lettered in wrestling and football. In the 10th grade, he began taking college classes and in the 11th grade, he was singing and dancing in the musical, "Carousel."

Finally, for all the families around the world who know the heartache of caring for an autistic child, there now existed a very real cause for hope.

Explanation of Visual Learning

Our world is a very verbal place. We use communication skills to read the paper in the morning, relate to our families, learn at school and exchange ideas at work. Communication is how we share our unique souls with the world and it is the most complex function of the human brain. In addition to words, we make great use of signs, symbols, gestures and even colors to communicate. Some people key in more to the visual aspects of life while others use their hearing more. You are reading the words this book without even thinking about it because it comes naturally to you, but for many in our society, it does not come easy or may even be impossible.

Communication difficulties can make it very hard to fit in socially, to thrive academically or to develop intimacy with loved ones. Without a proper understanding of written and spoken words, highly visual thinkers can be left without a common medium for communication with the rest of the world, leaving them isolated, confused and very frustrated. They are operating on a different level that just can't seem to connect with others, however hard they may be trying internally. This frustration and confusion can lead to anger, internal withdrawal or both, resulting in outward symptoms like temper tantrums or inward symptoms like unresponsiveness.

We often ask people to adjust to changes in schedule or plans by talking to them, often saying the same thing over and over when they don't seem to "get it." These words can create more confusion and frustration, as they may not be processed at the speed expected. Such people often complain they are being made to "feel stupid." As a result, normal word-based teaching methods are bound to fail.

Maverick Minds are highly visual thinkers who struggle when processing verbal language. They may have difficulty listening, reading, speaking or writing. Other symptoms may include behavioral, attention or memory issues. Often Mavericks seem to have symptoms of autism or Attention Deficit Disorder (ADD), which can mask or confound the underlying communication deficits.

What distinguishes a Maverick from other disorders is the highly visual brain and a specific cluster of 50 communication-related symptoms. Careful evaluation and training, however, can lead to fluent and successful communication and a reduction of symptoms that characterize autism or ADD. By treating the actual *cause*, the *symptoms* begin to disappear. Obviously, if a highly visual thinker is acting out because of frustration or anger at his or her inability to communicate, improvement in communication skills will bring great relief and joy.

Explanation of Visual Learning

Mavericks can seem like strangers in a strange land. They may not understand, think or speak in a language familiar to verbal people, but that does not mean they are not attempting to communicate. Individuals can function without a visual thinking system (such as those who are born blind), but living without a verbal system can be devastating. Being blind can cut you off from a world of things, but a verbal disorder cuts you off from the world of people.

When we say Mavericks are operating on a different level, this does not mean they function below the visual norm. In fact, they are actually on a quite advanced level that most of us don't understand. "Their gift is hidden by their disability," Dr. Florance says, "Maverick Minds often think a thousand times faster than their mouths can go." They communicate at such a high level through a world of mental pictures and videos that their verbal communication suffers. They may even enhance their visual ability by trying harder and harder to communicate in the only way they know how, causing an ever larger gap between their visual and verbal communication skills.

This is why Mavericks get so frustrated and upset at being told to do something over and over again or being told they aren't trying hard enough. They *are* trying as hard as they can and they are functioning at a very high level, but not in a way that most of us can recognize or understand.

In the Maverick Mind, the visual processing system is exponentially more powerful than the auditory one. Ohio State University Dean of Counseling and Tutoring Dr. John M. Stang, M.D. says, "The majority of the population has a balance between the two, but there is a small subset that are extraordinarily overdeveloped to the genius level in one, while the other fundamentally does not exist."

Fortunately, Dr. Florance found how to reach these Mavericks on their level. She developed a system called Brain Re-engineering that has helped thousands of Mavericks all over the world to build the verbal skills that allow them to communicate in our common *verbal* language, giving them the best of both worlds. Mavericks improve when the visual and verbal thinking systems are taught to work together in synergy as companion partners. When the verbal system becomes strong enough to work on its own, the Maverick becomes symptom free.

As complex language skills develop, so does an improvement in self control. As verbal abilities improve, children are better able to process information and express their needs. Language becomes a substitute for action.

This understanding has led to the popular "baby sign language" movement. A baby knows what it wants and desires to communicate long before verbal communication skills can develop. Children who are repeatedly shown the hand gesture for "bottle" or "milk" just before being given a bottle soon learn to make the gesture themselves to communicate their needs. Such children are known to cry less "for no reason," as they have a means to communicate their needs and desires before their physical capacity for verbal language develops.

When language development is abnormal, however, the development of behavioral control is disrupted. Unfortunately, many parents do not understand the connection between language development and a child's behavioral self control. Frequently children with language impairments are placed in situations where their ability to respond appropriately is compromised, not due to a lack of motivation or desire, but due to a lack of ability.

Parents and professionals often assume that a child who does not follow verbal reasoning nor comply with verbal instructions is *deliberately choosing* to not cooperate. When parents inadvertently continue to place pressure upon the language-disordered child to conform behaviorally, the child simply cannot understand, so it is not surprising that the child rebels or develops other behavioral problems. The language-disordered child cannot channel the frustration from failed attempts at following direction or expressing feelings or needs. This situation confuses adults when the child is at an age-appropriate level or excels in non-verbal areas.

Parental frustration and anger may then increase the language-impaired child's already significant level of frustration, leading to characteristic temper tantrums. Frequently treatment is directed at the child's misbehavior rather than the *cause* of that misbehavior, often precipitating a frustrating cycle of minimizing one behavior problem only to produce another. It is important for parents to recognize that delayed or deviant language development can lead to a wide range of behavioral and temperamental problems that do not respond to any of the usual parental discipline or therapeutic management techniques. Identification of language impairment as the true source of a child's problem is essential to determining the proper therapy.

Visual vs. Verbal

They say a picture is worth a thousand words and for the Maverick, this is literally true. When you read a description of a Van Gough painting or Michelangelo sculpture, you will have an idea of what it might look like, but the only way to know for sure is to see an image of it. Reception of knowledge through visual means is infinitely faster and more precise.

The problem is that visual images are great for receiving knowledge, but they are far less so for expressing knowledge. Maverick minds are so filled with rapidly sequencing visual images that words could never keep up. They literally speed past language in such a way that language does not properly develop. Once Whitney was able to express himself through pictures, whether it be the logo of his favorite French fry restaurant or later with pictures of words, he was able to channel his visual images through language to those around him. He was able to *communicate*. Communication cannot occur without some common ground for the intended message to be expressed and properly interpreted when received.

Some people have memories based on visual pictures in the mind, while others recall the voices of past conversations. Many authors, who obviously are more verbal than most people, will have "conversations" in their head with their characters or imagine conversations their characters have with each other before beginning to write a novel. They use words to conjure up images of characters, their surroundings and their lives.

As mentioned before, our emotional pathways often develop along our communication preferences. Like the two girls who reacted differently to the movie *Titanic*, our emotional pathways can be triggered by visual or verbal stimuli. Music is a highly important part of movies because of the reaction it can stimulate in an audience. If our verbal and visual perceptions are balanced, our experiences in life will be much richer, providing a wider range and understanding of emotions as well.

Visual Thinking and Memory

It would seem that one drawback to the visual/non-verbal mind is the lack of a mental filing cabinet. Computer programs have always been structured using a Directory Tree. Microsoft changed this to folders when they went to a more graphical representation with Windows, but the method of organizing information into a hierarchical structure remains the same. Bits of code or information are stored according to their location in the structure. Information is categorized within a context and associated by characteristics such as name, type, date created, date modified, purpose, etc. These categories and associations allow the information to be found and retrieved from the structure.

Without structure, without sequencing, without *language* and *words* that are put into an *order*, there can be no hierarchy, no associations between the information – and no way to retrieve an image from memory. It is verbal language which provides the structure wherein to place the pictures and later retrieve them. Without that structure, high visuals cannot remember and retain for long periods what they heard or saw. For the extreme Mavericks, they have excellent memory and recall of visual images (such as Whitney finding his way to the drug store for toys or to the hotel kitchen), but only so long as they can replay the same movie in their mind. Once the movie is over, the pictures are no longer accessible or retrievable. They are part of a stream of consciousness and a stream, by definition, cannot be captured or stored. It is constantly in motion.

The Maverick Mind

Mavericks are often misdiagnosed and misunderstood. Visual Mavericks think rapidly, which may cause them to appear inattentive or impulsive. At the same time, it may take a Maverick longer than most to answer a basic question because of the way they process information, but it appears to us in the verbal world that they lack focus. If they can't understand verbal reasoning, they may withdraw or become angry. If a Maverick is misunderstood by peers, significant others or family members, there may be an increase in symptoms. This topic is discussed in *A Parent's Guide: Language and Behavior Problems in Children* (1988, Goldstein, S. & Hinerman, P.).

Because behavioral symptoms are often seen as the primary problem, the therapist has no reason to investigate further. Once a diagnosis is made, it is rarely if ever questioned. A misdiagnosis precludes any possibility of discovering deficits in communication, which may be the true cause of the behavior.

Such a misdiagnosis can actually lead to problems with:

- Attention
- Motivation
- Compliance
- Withdrawal
- Anxiety
- Temper Tantrums
- Shutting Down

The highly visual maverick is often given many labels:

- Autism
- Attention Deficit Disorder (ADD)
- Pervasive Developmental Disorder
- Oppositional-Defiant Disorder
- Sleep Disorder
- Hyperactivity

The Autism Society and the *Ohio Handbook for the Identification, Evaluation, and Placement of Children with Language Problems* (1991, Ohio Department of Education) each list the following traits or symptoms common to autism.

These symptoms are remarkably similar as seen in the table below:

Autism Society	ODE Language Handbook
Insistence on sameness, resistance to change	Can't alter behavior according to the needs of a situation or setting. Perseverates, resistance to change
Difficulty in mixing with others	Relates poorly to peers, reluctant to participate, has few friends
Unresponsive to normal teaching methods	Unresponsive to normal teaching methods
Sustained odd play	Behaves immaturely and engages in odd play
Tantrums	Behavior problems

The same scenario is true for similarities in the symptoms of a communication disorder and ADD/ADHD:

Attention Deficit Disorder	ODE Language Handbook
Excessive verbal output	Talks a lot but says little
Lack of attention to the speaker	Offends listener, can't attend to discussion
Lack of compliance with commands	Can't follow directions
Failure to modulate social communication behaviors with shifting task demands	Can't alter behavior according to needs of the situation, audience or setting, trouble with transitions
Limited initiation of new themes	Limited initiation of new themes
Decreased frequency of responses to questions	Decreased frequency of responses to questions

What do the following groups have in common?

- Preschool children with language disorders
- School age speech/language language-impaired children
- Stutterers
- Brain damaged hospital patients

All of these populations have symptoms in attention, memory, listening, reading, writing or speaking. At the time Dr. Florance was researching stutterers, this disorder was thought to be a chronic, life-long disability. The fastest way to reach a symptom free goal was to teach new behaviors that would compete with stuttering and replace it. This led to similar training methods for the other groups that were very successful.

The same philosophy is behind Dr. Florance's treatment of autism. Her methods teach the attention, memory and communication skills that compete with autism to replace autistic symptoms. As a result, severe disability can be turned into lifelong ability. For the properly diagnosed patient, Dr. Florance can create individualized, step-by-step plans to reduce or eliminate symptoms.

 *Can it Really Work?*

Once it was understood that Maverick Minds were highly visual thinkers, it became clear that traditional verbal methods of communicating or teaching were bound to fail. The Mavericks simply could not connect on that level. A new method of communication and instruction had to be developed—one that could be understood and properly interpreted by the Maverick. The educational tools became pictures, videos and logos.

Case Studies

Beginning with her own son, Dr. Florance was able to draw a child out of his often-silent visual world into our world of people, sounds, and interaction. Despite this amazing success, one question remained: was Whitney truly a miracle in the sense that he was unique, or could the therapy produce similar results in other children? Was there finally hope for thousands of children and parents who were told no help was available?

Whitney

From the time he was born, Whitney did not respond to language. He could not bond with his family and could not recognize the people around him. Ultimately, he was diagnosed as an autistic and a severely handicapped—deaf and mute. Experts declared him unteachable.

Whitney's early years were very difficult. He did not seem to have normal emotional responses—there were no cuddles, leaving Dr. Florance hungry for the bonding she experienced with her two older children. She says of the time, "He had all of the symptoms of autism. He didn't know we were people. He didn't know what words were. He didn't relate to us at all. For years he didn't know he was a human being. It was as if he were hollow. He has no memory of those years. It must have been pretty vacant for him."

Dr. Florance began teaching Whitney non-verbally through his visual brain. He learned to read before he could hear or speak. His visual problem solving improved to that of an adult before he was able to use language to communicate. Then a bridge was formed to lead him to communication. He began to read with logos and used them to indicate his needs, like the time he showed his mother a picture of French fries to communicate that he was hungry.

The boy who seemed incapable of rational thought had been thinking all along, but in a different language—a language that was visual rather than verbal. Dr. Florance explains:

> *"I had been testing people's auditory and visual processes for over 20 years before Whitney was born. With stroke patients you can check to see if they can match a picture of a fork with the object, and if they can demonstrate what to do with it, and then if they can say the word. In other words, you try to see what connections are being made to replace or supplement their language system. Whitney was doing amazing things that were causing him to use visual attention and memory. He was actually problem solving -- independent of knowing we were people -- and not knowing words were words. But the first big thing I learned was the unparalleled power of the visual thinking engine."*

Once Dr. Florance made her breakthrough with Whitney, his life started to change for the better. He now enjoys a varied and exciting social life with family and friends and he has remained completely *symptom free*. With the help of the brain re-engineering process, Dr. Florance was able to successfully rewire her son's mind.

Sam

Sam was much like Dr. Florance's son, Whitney. He had poor verbal skills and was timid and shy in social situations because he could not understand words. He relied on his Mom and Dad—who were also visual thinkers—to translate into his language. Despite his problems, Sam appeared to be a visual genius. He memorized the alphabet and numbers by the age of two, and he could draw the world map by kindergarten.

While his visual talents could not be denied, Sam scored a 70 on his IQ test, placing him in the bottom two percentile at his age level. Sam and his mom, Cathy, worked with Dr. Florance to train Sam's visual brain to support his verbal processing system. Dr. Florance taught his brain processors to support listening, reading, writing and speaking. As therapy progressed, Sam's ADD symptoms resolved themselves. Sam's story is documented in the video "Anthony Analytic" at www.ebrainlabs.com. A year after working with Dr. Florance, Sam was functioning at or above his age level for all of his second grade skills. He has continued to blossom at every level.

Merea

Merea was diagnosed with autism at age two. She was quiet, almost non-verbal and did not play with other children. To communicate, she led her parents to what she wanted or needed. Merea also had severe tantrums and trouble maintaining a regular sleep pattern. She did not appear to be a typically happy two-year-old. She seldom smiled or laughed. Her parents were afraid to leave the house and avoided family get-togethers. Only one parent could go to her brother's sporting events because the other stayed home with Merea.

Despite these circumstances, her mother, Marleen, noted that Merea was able to use her visual thinking very easily. She could operate the VCR, play computer games, and put together intricate puzzles with ease. Her parents knew there was more to her symptoms than autism. Then Merea's mother read *Maverick Mind* and contacted Dr. Florance. Merea was able to learn self control as her attention and memory improved. Soon, she was able to comprehend verbal reasoning and she began talking to express herself. Merea's family is thrilled with the life-changing differences. Their daughter has progressed from tantrums and difficulty in communicating in her autism class, to a happy, healthy child working at or above her age level in a mainstream school.

Dr. T.C.

Not only children have benefitted from Dr. Florance's work. Dr. T.C. was a medical student struggling with the verbal deficits of a Maverick. She studied for 10-12 hours every day for 30 days to pass her Step One Board Examinations. Despite her efforts, she did not pass and was tested for learning disabilities at the recommendation of her professor. Although doctors thought she had ADD when she was young, no disabilities were found upon testing. So with the help of her professor, she prepared for the exam again. She also began the next step of her training, working along with supervisors at a teaching hospital. While her on-site evaluation was excellent, she still did not pass her board examinations and could not continue working at the hospital. With her career in serious jeopardy, she sought the help of Dr. Florance.

 *Case Studies*

Dr. T.C. was able to listen and read much more efficiently after working with the Brain Engineering program. A chapter that previously took her four hours to read with little retention or understanding now took 15 minutes and she was able to remember what she had read. She passed her examination and credits Dr. Florance for her success. Dr. T.C. hopes to help Mavericks like herself someday.

Caleb

In this picture, Caleb is learning to apply his Brain Engineering training so he can think in paragraphs and produce fluent, forward-moving speech. Caleb was diagnosed with autism as a very young child and had been in the special education classroom for many years. In the fall of his 6th grade year, his parents pulled him out of school because he was in such distress. They considered home schooling because his teachers felt Caleb would benefit most from reading pre-school picture books in a classroom by himself with one-on-one instructions. He was withdrawn and rarely spoke when he began working with Dr. Florance. When he did speak, he quoted lines from his favorite movies or made odd noises.

Early in Step 4 of the Brain Engineering process, Caleb's teacher felt he would respond well to preschool and early primary books. Several months later, he improved so much that he was mainstreamed for reading, science, spelling and social studies. He became a happy, competent verbal 6th grader, able to take notes and write his exams. He benefitted from working with the other students as well as his teachers, who were very proud of him. His school administration and teachers worked with his parents and Dr. Florance to build a strong support network for success.

Dr. L.B.

Dr. L.B. was referred to Brain Engineering Labs by her supervisors as a condition of continuing her residency. She required repeated instructions and had trouble sustaining attention during rounds at the hospital. She was also unable to pay attention while reading or listening to lectures. She was having trouble expressing herself and giving her bosses the correct information they needed. She was taking too long to finish her write-ups for patients and had trouble staying on schedule. Concern about losing her job created significant anxiety and lack of sleep. She was eventually asked to leave.

Dr. L.B. says Dr. Florance's help changed her life and enabled her to become the wonderful physician she was destined to become. She now is able to use both her superior visual and her excellent verbal thinking and communication systems. She created a presentation for her supervisors in which she explained how she met her goals and how she improved her sequencing and receptive/expressive language skills.

According to Dr. L.B.:

> *"Through your program, I have seen a difference in my efficiency in the office. I am doing mostly outpatient work and an elective rotation in Endocrinology this month. I see patients every 15-30 minutes and stay on time. My auditory attention has worked well to help me hear information the first time around. I have also been working with students and interns, and I use my output processors and associator constantly in order to teach medical management and OB management and procedures."*

As a result of her progress, Dr. L.B. was reinstated to the hospital. She was selected to represent her training program at meetings worldwide.

Seeing the visual thinker in a new light can change how everyone relates to them. This realization is a major first step in moving toward improvement. Sarando, an Adaptive Physical Education Teacher, from New York City, explains:

> *"Whitney's story has changed the way I see my students. I was watching a student get verbally harassed by my colleagues because he would not listen. The teacher would yell, "Daryl, stand on the balance board!" I said maybe he doesn't understand. I demonstrated what was expected using gestures and he did it right away. The teacher still thinks that Daryl was being defiant, but I am realizing that I have a lot of options. Yelling louder to a child who has breaks in his auditory connections can be really harmful."*

Joyce, another teacher, became aware of a common mistake that educators usually make. She says:

> *"I have to admit that I did see many students as lazy learners who just did not want to learn. However, I now see that they may be highly visual. We teach mostly through reading, writing, listening and speaking – which is our verbal pathway. Teachers like me must see that there are visual learners out there that have a hard time learning this way."*

Diagnosing the Maverick Mind

When properly diagnosed, Mavericks have an excellent prognosis and exhibit improvement from proper treatment immediately. To diagnose the Maverick mind, Dr. Florance conducts a Brain Engineering evaluation that includes:

- History Assessment
- eBrain Analysis of Risk (eAR)
- Visual Family Tree
- Florance Brain Print

History Assessment

The first step in assessing any potential Maverick is to gather information on the subject's history. What are his or her behaviors, abilities, difficulties, challenges? What are some notable events or incidents in their history? The best answers come from the parents, who tend to know their children best. Parents naturally monitor a child's strengths and weakness all the time with a mixture of hope, joy and fear, so they tend to recall specific incidents that gave them a sense of joy, pride or concern. Moreover, everyone in all countries and cultures begins the process of learning to communicate at home. Thus, an analysis of at-home skills is optimal not only for evaluation but for planning a training program as well. When guided by the proper questions, parents can be a wealth of very valuable information.

eBrain Analysis of Risk (eAR)

The eAR is a highly researched, complex 50-item assessment that measures attention/memory, listening, reading, speaking and writing to determine whether a person has visual or verbal dominance in the way they process and remember information. These are known as the "5 Clusters." Normal functioning children and adults will register on less than 15 of the 50 items as highly visual thinkers. To qualify as a Maverick Mind, at least 25 symptoms must be determined to be highly visual. Most Mavericks, however, register as highly visual on over 40 items, many on all 50. These are people with a highly visual way of interacting with the world and low verbal skills.

Mavericks tend to have a family history of highly visual brains in the family tree, which leads us to the next assessment: potential progress. If at least one parent is a highly visual thinker, then the probability of improvement with therapy increases dramatically—even with adopted children.

Visual Family Tree

In this assessment, we analyze the family tree for visual thinkers. It is our most critical predictor of success. Normal functioning children and adults may have no visual thinkers in their family history, while Mavericks have a distinct pattern within their family tree. Fourteen-year-old Tina, who seemed to have symptoms of attention deficit syndrome, had two highly visual parents. John, who did not speak for 15 years, had three generations of visual thinkers in his family tree.

VISUAL FAMILY TREE
Prognosis Predictor

Family History	Prognosis
No history	Poor
Some visuals in family tree	Marginal
1 visual parent	Good
2 visual parents	Excellent!

As you can see from the table above, the greater the visual ability of the family, the greater the prognosis for success. This does not mean that a non-visual family is without hope, but they will have to learn more to be effective for the child. Visual thinkers understand the same "language," so to speak, so visual-thinking family members are better equipped to work with Mavericks to help and support them in their therapy.

Visual people communicate differently within the home and tend to create more visually-oriented leisure time activities. In addition, approaches to homework, chores, and shared experiences are different in the visual family. A visual family can have an entirely different worldview, customs, habits and conversational patterns that are quite unique. Once he overcame his own handicaps, Whitney was able to communicate more effectively with other Mavericks than most verbal thinkers. It was like they were part of a club with a unique understanding of each other because they interpreted the world around them in a similar manner.

In working with over 1,000 visual families, in every case at least one parent was highly visual. Both parent and child think in a world of color and images rather than words. These parents are in fields like engineering, architecture, medicine, computers, art and business. They are extremely capable of intelligent thought and communication, but they think in pictures first and then convert to words. The autistic child may have visuals that are overworking to the point that language is under-developed or (as in Whitney's case) non-existent, so the visual parent is better able to reach them.

Prognosis for Success

Over the years, Dr. Florance has developed several indicators to predict expected progress. These Prognosis Predictors are based on thousands of cases and the common factors that emerged in dealing with Maverick Minds and their families.

Readiness for Change Profile

Parents and family are an important part of any therapy plan, as they are included as trainers. Each family has its own unique, specific culture of change, and we learn to communicate within that culture in different ways that can affect potential progress. Certain family characteristics have been proven to create a more favorable environment for therapy, as shown in the Readiness for Change Profile chart below:

Readiness for Change Profile

Family History	Prognosis
High empathizer	Excellent
Internal locus of control	Excellent
Opportunity focus	Excellent
Positive explanatory	Excellent

Because the goal is symptom-free communication, the communication style of the parents/trainers is crucial to success. Parents who empathize with their child's thoughts and feelings are great at monitoring and reporting progress, but are often not capable of initiating positive change because they are focused on the child's current abilities or immediate feelings and may feel trapped by fate. Parents who have an internal locus of control believe their actions can cause change, but they focus on the problem instead of the solution. Parents who

find opportunities to create learning experiences tend to fare better than those who focus on the problem. Parents who intuitively speak in a positive explanatory style tend to be the best trainers.

There are clusters of teachable skills which are best learned with parental and familial involvement. It is critical that the child learn intuitive attention, memory, listening, reading, speaking and writing within this natural context. The extent to which the parents themselves can learn and develop the kind of training skills required has a direct impact on the child becoming symptom free. Based on the progress achieved, progress and therapy can be reevaluated and new goals established.

The Ideal Candidate

As with any therapy, progress will be determined by the individual's capabilities and the degree to which a therapy program is followed. Based upon decades of experience, Dr. Florance has found the following indicators offer the best prognosis for the quickest success:

- At least a 50% score on the eBrain Analysis of Risk (the higher the score, the better the prognosis)
- High number of visual thinkers in the Family Tree (especially parents)
- A high score on the Readiness for Change Profile

General Discussion

Words are not thoughts. They are *expressions* of thoughts. If you grew up in France, you would learn to express your thoughts in French. If you grew up in Italy, you would learn to express your thoughts in Italian. In all cases, however, the existence of thoughts precedes the ability to learn how to express them. People who learn another language know what it means to transition from merely translating words or phrases from your own language into the words of the new language, to the point where you are actually able to think thoughts in the new language using that language's words. This is what is meant by being "conversational" when you learn a new language. You are able to express your thoughts directly using the words of a foreign language.

Now imagine you have thoughts but *no* words. None whatsoever. You have a language completely made up of pictures – pictures that are *received* but cannot be *expressed*. You can see and recognize a box of Lucky Charms cereal by the cute little leprechaun on the package, but you cannot *express* the picture of a leprechaun. You might be able to draw it, but that is not the same as *expression*. A drawing is a *representation* of something, not an expression.

When we say, "express yourself" in art, we actually refer to the act of creating something artistic, but it is the *act* that is the expression, not the painting or sculpture left behind. Dance and music are expressions through movement or the manipulation of sound using an instrument, but it is the *act* of dancing or playing music that is the expression. When a performance is through, nothing remains of the creative act itself! If there is a video or audio recording, we can see only the results of what had been expressed, but even then, we neither feel the feelings nor the creativity of the artist, we only see or hear the *results* of their expression through another medium. These expressions may trigger in us similar feelings that the artist wishes to convey, but we feel *our* feelings, based on *our* experiences. The art is simply a form of language that use common experiences and thoughts to triggers feelings – a language with no words but with a structure that is recognized by both the audience and the artist.

Now imagine you have a picture in your mind of the Trix rabbit. You want a bowl of Trix, but your world includes no words. You could draw it, if you knew and understood what a pen and paper was for, but if you are a child like Whitney who had no motor skills to control a pen, how would you express the image of the Trix rabbit to others so they understand? You *can't!* It's *impossible!* The picture of the Trix rabbit exists only in your mind! There is no way to connect your inner image of the Trix rabbit with the image inside the mind of another person without some common reference point – and we call that common reference point "language." Now imagine that the entire world only exists as pictures in your mind. You have no means to distinguish the image of the Trix rabbit from any other image in your world: your brothers,

sisters—even your own father and mother. The Trix rabbit would be no more or less real to you than your own mother, just one more common, repetitive image in a world of images.

Now at some point, you will realize there is *something* different about your mother. The Trix rabbit doesn't give you food or drink. The picture you associate as mom has the ability to give you things you want: a toy, pizza, turn on the TV. But *the picture that is mom* is inherently frustrating, because *the picture that is mom* doesn't give you what you want when you want it, and there is no way to know when – if ever – *the picture that is mom* will give you what you want again. Unable to express your thoughts to convey your wishes, and being unable to understand the world around you, you may withdraw into yourself and babble or sing or wave your hands, or you may scream and bite and throw a tantrum. It's all the same to you. It makes no difference. Nothing matters.

This is the world of the autistic child, who is often an extremely intelligent little person with a mind that is racing but with no method of communication – no *language*. They have no concept of "odd behavior" because they have no concept of their effect on anything around them. The worst part is—because they *are* thinking and *are* aware of the world around them but are unable to communicate with that world, unable to express themselves, ask for something or ask why they are not allowed to do something they want —their lives are filled with frustration.

They get involved with something important to them and then they are forced to stop. They don't know why. They want something and cannot get it. They don't know why. We think their behavior makes no sense to us, but it is *our* world that makes no sense to them.

This explains the need for routine. Since life without verbal reasoning seems chaotic to the autistic child, routine helps them develop a sense of security. They can relax somewhat knowing that at a certain time of day, the same thing is going to happen. It takes some of the unpredictability and fear out of their lives. They know they will see a movie at night, they will be fed in the morning, and so on. It doesn't remove all frustration from their lives, but it helps.

The world is filled not only with thousands of pictures we take for granted every day, but with thousands of variations of those pictures: shadows, colors, lighting, movement, etc. If you look at a wall, you will say, "That wall is white," or "That wall is blue," but neither statement is true. Look at any wall closely and you will see thousands of color changes as the sun streams in a window, a light brightens a portion of the wall, a shadow darkens another part of the wall. Add any sort of texture to the wall and you get a million highlights, lowlights and shadows. We normally filter these things out as unimportant, but the visual child does not.

They see it all and want to explore it all in infinite detail. This is the visual attention zoom lens in action.

Without any basis for communication, our reasoning and actions make no sense to the autistic child. As a result, their lives are filled with mounting frustration and they react the only way they can: by either throwing a fit or withdrawing from our world entirely into themselves. Their lives become one long silent scream.

The problem of reaching these "other world" children is compounded by the attitudes and practices of many in the therapeutic community. These children are tested according to our world, not theirs, so they are bound to fail and are labeled as deficient. They are asked to comply with spoken verbal directions, but they are only able to think or communicate in pictures, so they inevitably score low. The IQ test does test thinking ability in a wide variety of areas, but common practice is to then combine all the scores and average them out. This practice is in direct contradiction to the intent of the man who developed the test, a Frenchman named Albert Binet.

Monsieur Binet published the first intelligence test in 1905, and it is the basis of the IQ test we use today. His goal was to identify children who needed extra help in school to target their weak areas – not to have his test used as a basis for excluding children who were "unteachable." German psychologist and philosopher Wilhelm Louis Stern adjusted Binet's formulas and in 1916, Lewis Terman published his own version as the Stanford-Binet IQ test while he was a professor of cognitive psychology at Stanford University. It is interesting to note that Professor Terman was (like Darwin, Margaret Sanger, and Hitler) an avowed Eugenicist, meaning the human race should be "purified" by restricting the "right" of people to procreate unless they were able to produce children that were not "defective."

Professor Terman was a member of the Human Betterment Foundation, which was established in Pasadena, California to lobby for compulsory sterilization laws in the United States that would force "undesirables" to be sterilized for eugenic purposes. For many like Margaret Sanger and Hitler, "undesirables" could mean the poor, blacks, Jews, or anyone else the elite deemed humanly defective. These people were hardly concerned with helping children who did not appear to be "normal." They literally felt these children were, as Margaret Sanger put it , "...human beings who should never have been born." In *Women and the New Race* (Eugenics Publ. Co., 1920, 1923), Sanger further advocated, "The most merciful thing that a large family does to one of its infant members is to kill it." You can imagine what the fate of any autistic child would have been, had this group been successful.

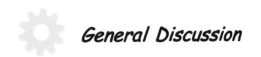 *General Discussion*

Society has traditionally believed that the more verbal you are in the early years, the smarter you are. Professor Terman developed a special training program for gifted children (as measured by his IQ tests), who nicknamed themselves "Termites." He groomed these children with all sorts of special educational advantages and they consistently scored well on tests. Similar programs have sprung up all across America, from Hunter College High School in New York to the GATE (Gifted and Talented Education) program in California. However, because everyone *assumes* such programs work, very few studies have ever been done to verify the programs' success. In fact, Terman's Termites did *not* do nearly as well as he had hoped and he was at a loss to explain this.

Joanna Schaffhausen, a graduate student at Yale University studying the cellular mechanisms of learning and memory, studied the results of Dr. Terman's experiment. Her findings in an article titled, "Child Prodigies," is published online at: www.brainconnection.positscience.com.

"Terman was quite surprised to find that starting life with an enormous IQ was no guarantee of future success. While it was true most of his subjects went on to make substantial contributions to society, there were many who seemed to flounder as they reached adulthood. Some had trouble keeping a steady job, others were merely average at the jobs they had. The Termites' intellectual prowess did not make them immune to mental illness, and a good percentage struggled with alcoholism. At least twenty-two of his subjects committed suicide. Terman searched his early data for clues that might explain why some of his children succeeded where others failed, but he was unable to find any reliable predictors. Furthermore, none of Terman's subjects achieved the kind of fame or made the genius contributions that he had hoped they would. Terman was correct that precociously bright children grow up to be bright adults, but IQ is not necessarily the best measure of a person's potential. Among the students passed over for Terman's study, there were two Nobel laureates. Among Terman's group, there were none."

Fortunately, not all psychologists bought into this philosophy. In 1969, Samuel A. Kirk and John N. Paraskevopoulos published *The Development and Psychometric Characteristics of the Revised Illinois Test of Psycholinguistic Abilities* (University of Illinois Press). They rebelled against the view (which is still considered mainstream today) that overall intelligence is the average of the parts. They agreed with Binet that if you could identify specific areas of weakness in a child (for example: thinking, vocabulary, attention, memory or problem solving) a school could target those specific areas of weakness. Binet had created a school for "mental orthopedics" along these lines, but when his methods were imported into the United States,

American psychologists of the day *did not believe* you could do anything to *improve* individual problem areas, so they lumped all the scores together and averaged them out. For decades since, the majority of American mental therapists have not looked for answers for children with low IQ scores because they were predisposed by their training to believe there was no possibility of improvement. If you were pigeon-holed into a category of "low-functioning" mental ability, you were lost there forever.

Kirk and Paraskevopoulos were dissatisfied with this lumping of children into one category. They found that among this group, children had a wide variety of capabilities. A child may have a specific weakness in one area, but be very strong in others. They decided to breakdown the testing into measurements of distinct mental processing systems, including communication routes like receptive language processing, expressive language processing and the internal thought process of organizing and interpreting.

These tests were able to reveal when a child had a big difference in their auditory and visual processing. In other words: if they were highly visual thinkers or not. Both auditory and visual processing must be present and work together to communicate in our world. Words are perceived visually when read and are usually associated with what the word sounds like when heard. There must also be a correlation with the *meaning* of the word.

If a child is a highly visual thinker, he or she may recognize the word or its meaning by looking at it but be unable to speak it. By using targeted tests such as this, it is possible for a therapist to determine which area is weakest and use the stronger area as a tool to reach and improve the weaker skill. This sort of targeted assessment becomes impossible if all skills are lumped together, just as it is when all children are lumped together into one category despite their many individual strengths and weaknesses.

Around the time Whitney was six years old, Dr. Florance discovered another book that was to give her independent confirmation of her theories, *Psychiatric and Behavioral Characteristics of Children with Communication Disorders*, written by Dennis P. Cantwell and Lorian Baker. Dr. Cantwell literally "wrote the book" on psychiatric disorders. He was a contributing author to the DSM, the Diagnostic Statistical Manual of Mental Disorders, which was used to diagnose psychiatric disease. He began to question the extent to which children diagnosed with psychiatric disease might actually suffer from a communicative disorder. He conducted an exhaustive research of literature in the field and concluded it was unreliable.

In science-speak, the doctor explained:

"Unfortunately, much of the literature in this area suffers from a lack of objective methods and operational diagnostic criteria for psychiatric disorder; confounding of the psychiatric and communication disorder variables; lack of operational diagnostic criteria for both the presence and type of communication disorder; use of unrepresentative samples for study (e.g., use of children with communication disorders who have who have been referred to a psychiatric facility); and lack of appropriate control groups."

In other words, despite all of the assumptions that been taught for decades, the so-called experts in the field had been sloppy in their research and the results could not be trusted. It was unknown to what extent communication disorders had led to learning disabilities or psychiatric misdiagnosis. None of the "known" assumptions in this area could be trusted!

The doctor's insight to the possibility that communication problems might lead to psychiatric symptoms began with his trip to London. Coming from Los Angeles, Dr. Cantwell had anticipated no problems with conducting research in another English-speaking country. Unskilled at deciphering the wide variety of British accents, however (many of which are unintelligible even to other Brits), he found himself wandering around a train station in London asking people where he needed to go to catch his train. Frustrated by his inability to speak effectively or comprehend what he was told, he noticed that he himself had begun exhibiting many of the "psychiatric disorders" that he had treated in others. Inwardly, he was anxious and sad, while outwardly he appeared to others as non-compliant, defiant, and oppositional. This world-renowned professor felt panic at the thought of being lost in a system he didn't understand, with no way to communicate with those around him.

Dr. Cantwell's conclusion was like a lightning bolt to Dr. Florance:

*"Learning disordered children cannot be considered to be a homogeneous subgroup. Most suffer from concurrent disorders of reading, spelling, and arithmetic. The overlap of deficits and **visual-spatial skills** renders 'pure' learning disorders unlikely. Early communication disorders are likely precursors to developmental learning disorders."*

In other words, communication problems existed *before* the learning disabilities. All "learning disordered" children were *not* the same. This was certainly proven with Whitney. Dr. Cantwell had also noticed a correlation to visual spatial skills.

Measuring the Brain Thinking Pathways

We have five senses, including the two primary senses of Seeing and Hearing and the auxiliary senses of Touch, Taste and Smell. Our primary senses are used to form thoughts by moving stimuli from the sense organ of Eyes and Ears through attention to memory to knowledge. The Eye-to-Brain pathway is called the *Opticoder* and the Ear-to-Brain Pathway is called the *Lexicoder*. If the Opticoder is overworking—meaning that the picture Brain is dominating—it can become the enemy of the Lexicoder and cause a lack of sensory integration between the two primary systems. As a result, a lack of integration can then occur in the other senses as well (such as when Whitney's arm was pinned yet he felt no pain). As the two pathways begin to work together, the rest of the senses begin to work properly as well.

Sequencing & Associating

Visual people often use association to form memories. When they learn a new idea, they relate that idea to their own knowledge base. The opposite of the brain's *associator* is the verbal pathway, or *sequencer*. The sequencer is rigid and ordering, enabling us to think in paragraphs. The associator is time-independent and the sequencer is very time-based. Understanding consequences depends on time-based processing of cause and effect.

Whitney, at age 4, wanted to jump off the roof to fly like Superman. He didn't understand the danger involved because he had no understanding of cause and effect. Whitney would also sit mesmerized watching Disney's Snow White as if he were deaf. The fire alarm bell would send him into a fit, yet at other times you could scream in his ear and he would hear nothing. At these times, the verbal processing of his brain was being shut down by the over-activity of his visual processing. A sense of cause and effect can only be developed if you have an ability to correlate information. If life is simply a series of recurring images with no ability to correlate them (language), then there can be no correlation between cause and effect and children can engage in dangerous behavior with literally no concept of the potential danger.

Often Mavericks feel that they must complete a pattern to finish a thought. If the thought process is disrupted, the Maverick may hit a wall and resort to talking with lines from a movie or echoing what was said, getting stuck like a broken record. Remember Whitney's question, "If she wants me to learn about the Civil War, why does she interrupt me when I am halfway understanding something and tell me to do something else? I will forget what I have read and have to read it over again."

 *General Discussion*

Expressive Communication

The associator can lead a Maverick to create messages that are difficult for the rest of us to understand. Mark, a college student diagnosed with autism, was asked, "How did you get here today?" He replied as follows:

> *"I took the train in from Long Island. My family went to the beach. Maybe I will be an engineer. The reason I like engineering is that there are serious problems. I have always been good in math. When teachers are difficult to understand. Like Dr. Einstein. There was an exhibit on Einstein at the history museum. Did you see it?"*

This seemingly disjointed speech is based on the association of visual images. In his attempt to communicate, there was no way to express the visuals inside his mind, so he jumped from one interior picture to another without using words to communicate the association. For Mark, internally, these associations were self-evident. For the rest of us, any association seems non-existent.

Here is a "translation" into sequencer language that most of us would understand:

> *"I took the train in from Long Island. The train reminds me of a picture in my mind from the time my family took me to the beach and we rode the train. A train is designed by people who are mechanical engineers. Maybe I will be an engineer. The reason I like engineering is that there are serious problems to solve that require math skills. I have always been good in math, except at times when my math teachers were difficult to understand. I recently saw a video on Dr. Albert Einstein and learned that he had a hard time understanding his teachers, too. There was an exhibit on Einstein at the history museum. Did you see it?"*`

Brittany, a high school Maverick, viewed the movie *Pearl Harbor*, with a highly verbal friend. Brittany was stunned. Her friend shed tears when the romance of the characters hit a speed bump, which was explained through a verbal exchange. Brittany thought the scenes that deserved the tears were the ones involving fighter planes at war, because people were dying. Crying during the war scenes seemed misplaced to her friend but was very logical to Brittany.

Tom, an adult physician Maverick, says that his emotions always hit much later after an event. He will cry or laugh long after the real time experience has passed. He processes the implications much later. This is a real world example of an old joke from the 1940's, "Don't tell him a joke on Saturday night or he'll laugh in church the next morning." Obviously, someone laughing or crying for no apparent reason can make that person seem odd, insensitive, or inappropriate to others.

Having a communication disorder can result in a very complex life socially, academically and vocationally. Having worked with children and adults who have trouble processing and producing language for nearly 40 years, Dr. Florance is very sympathetic to their daily frustration, anxiety, tension and disappointment.

The Complexities of Language

Children develop basic language skills from birth to about 4th grade. Although they develop at vastly different rates with unique profiles, the Mavericks develop in ways far different than what are considered normal. Because of this odd developmental profile, parents can be confused by symptoms, unsure about diagnostic labels, frustrated with test results and worried about what to do. Mavericks are often misunderstood, misdiagnosed and mismanaged.

In general, we evaluate disorders by comparing the chief complaint with subjective and objective data. Collecting data directly from a child with a communication disability can be very complex because they may have difficulties with verbal reasoning and sequencing, which are necessary to answer questions and follow verbal instructions. Being in a new situation with unfamiliar professionals can also create enormous anxiety. Familiar cues and contexts that could be helpful are removed. As a result, parents often feel that their children have more potential than is demonstrated in the exam room. Of course, extreme visual thinkers who have limited ability to understand or respond to spoken language will be able to offer little (if any) useful information.

Eighty percent of Mavericks exhibit symptoms related to *receptive language* (listening and reading). Prior to therapy, Mavericks could recall an average of seven words from a story in 30 seconds, needed to hear questions repeated at work, and their supervisors were concerned about keeping them employed at their companies. After training and therapy, they could accurately recall an average of 200 words from a story in three minutes, with little or no repetition.

Eighty percent of Mavericks also have difficulty with e*xpressive language* (speaking and writing). Prior to therapy, they used a lot of negative words to describe their lack of confidence. They were very anxious about making spoken presentations and left out important details. After therapy, they felt competent and confident in their speaking ability and received great feedback for their accuracy and relevance.

 *General Discussion*

Food for Thought and Discussion

Clearly, both receptive and expressive language are essential to success in school and in the workplace. Dr. Florance has helped literally thousands of people to improve their lives by helping them develop their verbal brain skills to balance out their visual skills. The following are quotes from a variety of sources that relate to these concepts:

> *"In elementary school, 75% of classroom instruction is auditory. By high school, instruction is 95% auditory. Auditory processing is the brain's organizational system."*
> —Ohio Department of Education Task Force on Language, 1992

> *"Learning a second language offers insight about the language-impaired. Most of us are intuitive language users. We do not actually learn to listen, speak, read, or write. These are specific pre-programmed functions. The brain's computer for language malfunctions in 20% of children and adults."*
> —Learning Disabilities Association, 1992

> *"Children with untreated language disorders have a 95% chance of having reading, writing, and spelling problems by age 9. Early language treatment is needed to change these odds."*
> —Donald Tower, M.D., National Institutes of Health

> *"Changing the way the brain works to use language is very complex. The design of therapy takes careful planning by experts. Each element of the therapy must be organized with attention to the emotional and behavioral response of the patient."*
> —George Shames, Ph.D. Clinical, Psychologist, 1980

> *"Communication disorder affects self esteem. We learn to see ourselves as winners as we interact verbally with others and are reinforced."*
> —Frank E. New, The ODE Language Handbook, 1991

> *"Neurological language impairments such as attention, memory, or processing disorders are caused by congenital malformation of the language centers in the brain. Although educational problems can result, the cause of the problem is not an educational or learning disorder."*
> —"The Neurological Basis of Language Disorder," NIH Monograph

"The neurological weakness for auditory processing begins before birth. By age 4, 60% of language-impaired children present symptoms of Psychiatric Disease. Early language therapy can prevent the onset of these devastating symptoms."

—Dennis Cantwell, M.D., UCLA

"Juvenile delinquents have an 80% chance of having a language disorder. Poor processing can lead to unintentional lying, frustration, humiliation, and embarrassment. The anger that results can lead to drug and alcohol problems or difficulty with compliance with rules at home or at school."

— Canada Journal of Language Speech and Hearing in Schools, July 1992

"Our knowledge of the brain and language has dramatically improved in the last 10 years. As we are able to better pinpoint the specific cause of the disorder, then we can design tightly organized and effective treatment."

—Dennis Cantwell, MD, 1992

"Language impaired patients have difficulty predicting the consequences of their actions. Impulsive behavior results. Language therapy helps to strengthen the sequential thinking needed to weigh alternatives and handle thought options. Coping and compliance improve as language improves."

—The Neurology, Learning and Behavior Center, Salt Lake City

The human language system is essential to every daily act. The demands on our brain's language computer change from year to year. The books we read in second grade are very different from those in sixth grade. Everyone should have an annual language physical. Language impairments that are not treated get worse and can be life damaging."

—Dennis Cantwell, 1991

"In the 1990s, treatment to improve post-stroke language is routine in most hospitals. For children, the neurological aspects of the language disorder require treatment that addresses the etiology of the disorder. Therapy in conjunction with school-based services, for example, offers a good marriage of treating both the neurological causes and the educational symptoms."

—Ron Goldman, Ph.D., 1993

"Language disorders have been under-treated in the past. Language impairments affect 15-20% of the adult population. Problems identified at age 4 were still present at age 34."

—Journal of Speech, Language, and Hearing Research, 1992

General Discussion

"What does education often do? It makes a straight-cut ditch of a free meandering brook. The significant problems we face cannot be solved at the same level of thinking we were at when we created them."

—Albert Einstein

"Never doubt that a small group of thoughtful committed citizens can change the world; indeed it is the only thing that has."

—Margaret Mead

"Thought is the blossom, language is the bud, and action is the fruit behind it."

—Ralph Waldo Emerson

"All that you are is the result of all that you have thought."

—Buddha

"My grace is perfect for you. For power is made in perfect weakness."

—Jesus

"We make a living by what we get, but we make a life by what we give."

—Winston Churchill (severe stutterer)

"Try not to become a man of success but rather a man of value."

—Albert Einstein

The 5 Steps of Brain Engineering

As communication skills improve, autistic symptoms tend to decrease, which then allows for even more improvement. Dr. Florance's Brain Engineering therapy follows a progressive model to build skill upon skill in five steps:

Step 1: Attention & Memory: the Brain Pillars

Step 2: Self Control: Anchoring the Central Executive

Step 3: Listening and Reading: Developing Input Processors

Step 4: Speaking and Writing: Developing Output Processors

Step 5: Self Esteem: Home, School and Work

Attention and Memory: the Brain Pillars

In Step 1, Mavericks learn to use their highly intuitive and powerful visual attention and memory systems to access their auditory attention and memory. This allows them to form a solid foundation for learning. Many of the symptoms of autism and ADD stem from weakness in listening, receptive language and verbal memory skills.

Self Control: Anchoring the Central Executive

In Step 2, training is aimed at teaching the skills that build self control over mood, behavior and communication, which are controlled by the brain's *central executive*. The drivers of the central executive are the *sequencer* and the *associator*. The sequencer is the driving engine of all language. It is very rigid and unforgiving. Only one word can be interpreted at a time and words must be received in a specific order for meaning to be conveyed. Words need to flow in a very specific order to create a sentence, sentences must flow to create paragraphs, and paragraphs must build sequentially to convey a larger message.

By contrast, the very powerful associator of the visual brain can think in many patterns all at once, like a surgeon who is aware of all internal organs while performing a heart operation, monitoring lung function, pulse, blood pressure and temperature all at the same time. For a Maverick to become efficient in using language, he or she must develop the ability to channel switch between the visual and the verbal brain. The central executive allows such channel switching to help prioritize, plan and translate thoughts into words.

Listening and Reading: Developing Input Processors

In Step 3, Mavericks learn the receptive language skills of listening and reading. This is how human beings move knowledge into the brain. By anchoring the central executive, Mavericks are able to use their brain support to control how they manage information. Fluency in thinking and communicating comes from the efficiency in which new ideas move from immediate recall to short term memory to long term memory. By improving attention and memory as well as channel switching between verbal and visual processing, Mavericks are able to move toward a symptom free life.

Speaking and Writing: Developing Output Processors

In Step 4, Mavericks use the strength of their receptive language to support speaking and writing. We learn through our receptive language but we are graded by our expressive language. All our lives we rely on our receptive language to help us encode our ideas from thought to word, yet our expressive language is how we are measured on tests, at work or at school. Many of the symptoms of autism or ADD are measured by how someone answers questions or knows how to say the right thing at the right time.

Self-Esteem: Home, School and Work

In Step 5, Mavericks build self esteem to meet the ultimate goal: successful interaction at home, school and work. Mavericks tend to be highly intuitive and big picture thinkers. Often Mavericks work from the concept to the details. They associate. Although these traits can cause problems initially, when harnessed properly they allow the Maverick to excel. At first, they will need to *transfer* their new skills to various structured situations with special support or accommodation. *Generalization* occurs when the skill becomes a fully functioning automatic habit that no longer relies on support. Once a Maverick is generalized at home, school and work, they are considered to be mainstreamed.

How to Evaluate Your Child

If you have been told your child is autistic, has ADD, or you suspect there may be a communication problem, use the following questionnaire to evaluate your child. Simply answering a questionnaire is no substitute for an accurate diagnosis, but if you answer yes to 50% or more of the questions below, you should pursue further diagnosis.

For more information, visit www.ebrainlabs.com or email Dr. Florance at braindr@cheriflorance.com.

The Maverick Child
eBrain Analysis of Risk

Indicate below the responses that describe you:	Yes - many	Some	None
Does anyone in your family have a job as an architect, doctor, engineer, mechanic, landscaper, artist, computer analyst, musician, or similar careers?	○	○	○
	Yes	**Sometimes**	**No**
Do you see pictures when you read?	○	○	○
Can you visualize a cupcake? Put a candle in it? See the candle lit? See it with pink icing?	○	○	○

Continued next page

The Maverick Child
eBrain Analysis of Risk

Indicate below the responses that describe your child.	Yes	Sometimes	No
Does your child seem smarter than he or she is able to demonstrate on tests?	O	O	O
Does your child prefer reading instructions to hands-on learning?	O	O	O
Does your child like to set the agenda in play?	O	O	O
Does your child like playing with Legos, puzzles, computer games, or sports equipment?	O	O	O
Does your child have a short attention span, except when watching his/her favorite T.V. shows?	O	O	O
Does your child like to watch a particular section of a video over and over?	O	O	O
Does your child make and keep friends easily?	O	O	O
If you try to use verbal reasoning, does your child throw a temper tantrum?	O	O	O
Does your child go into his/her own world?	O	O	O
Does your child have problems when asked to adapt to change quickly?	O	O	O
Does your child remember how to find places you have driven to?	O	O	O
Does your child prefer movies to books?	O	O	O
Does your child become hyper or withdrawn in noisy places?	O	O	O
Does your child have trouble falling asleep?	O	O	O
Does your child tune out when listening?	O	O	O
Does your child have trouble with verbal learning at school?	O	O	O
Is your child frustrated when trying to communicate?	O	O	O